Two Concepts of the Soul in Plato's *Phaedo*

A Beginner's Guide to the *Phaedo* and Some Related Platonic Texts on the Immortality of the Soul

Ryan Topping

UNIVERSITY PRESS OF AMERICA,® INC.
Lanham • Boulder • New York • Toronto • Oxford

Copyright © 2007 by
University Press of America,® Inc.
4501 Forbes Boulevard
Suite 200
Lanham, Maryland 20706
UPA Acquisitions Department (301) 459-3366

PO Box 317
Oxford
OX2 9RU, UK

All rights reserved

British Library Cataloging in Publication Information Available

Library of Congress Control Number: 2006923097
ISBN-13: 978-0-7618-3401-4 (paperback)
ISBN-10: 0-7618-3401-X (paperback)

Contents

Acknowledgments	v
Preface	vii
List of Abbreviations	ix

1 General Introduction — 1
  The Scope of this Book — 1
  Four Aspects of the *Concept* of the Soul — 2
  Two Concepts of the ψυχή in the *Phaedo* — 3
  Structure of the Book — 4

2 The Basic Concept of the ψυχή in the *Phaedo* — 9
  Introduction — 9
  Division of the Subject Matter of the Text of the *Phaedo* — 10
  Features of the ψυχή Not Used as the Basis for Arguments for Immortality — 12
  Conclusion: Statement of the *Basic* Concept of the ψυχή — 17

3 The Concept of the ψυχή in the *Phaedo*:
  Features in Addition to the Basic Concept — 19
  Introduction — 19
  Four Arguments Intended to Prove the ψυχή Will Survive Death and Exist Forever — 20
  1st Argument: Generation from Opposites (70C-72E) — 21
  2nd Argument: Learning as Recollection (72E-77D) — 23
  3rd Argument: The ψυχή is Similar to the Forms and to Divinity (78B-80D) — 25

4th Argument: The ψυχή as the Principle of Life will not Admit its Opposite (102B-106E)	26
The ψυχή of the Genuine Philosopher in the Afterlife (80D-84B; 114C-E)	29
How the True Philosopher Lives in this Life: Philosophy is the Training for Death	31
Conclusion: The *total* concept of the ψυχή in the *Phaedo*	34

4 Alternative Treatments of the ψυχή in Some of Plato's 'Middle' Dialogues — 39

Introduction	39
Meno: Recollection as the Basis for Showing the immortal ψυχή	39
Symposium: Vicarious Immortality and the Search for the Beautiful	40
Republic: The ψυχή is Immortal and Has Three Parts	42
Phaedrus: The Tripartite ψυχή is an Unmoved Mover	45
Conclusion: Alternative Treatments of the ψυχή Contrasted with the *Phaedo*	46

5 General Conclusion — 51

Summary of the Findings of this Study	51
The Moral Value of Socrates' Arguments for the Immortality in the *Phaedo*	54
Bibliography	59
Index	61

Acknowledgments

I would like to thank Don McCarthy, James Muir, Kevin Shroeder, Gillian Rathbone, and Fr. David Meconi S.J., who read drafts of this book and gave many helpful suggestions. Financial contributions, which are gratefully acknowledged, were also made by Pembroke College, Oxford, at a latter stage of the writing.

I want to thank our friends who lived at or around the Emmaus House Community, Winnipeg, Canada, which my wife and I were part of during the period which this manuscript first took shape.

In te, Domine, speravi: non confundar in aeternum.

Preface

As indicated by the title my aim has been to provide a guide that will help the beginner who has a dedicated interest in the *Phaedo* to come to a deeper understanding of the structure of the text and some of the arguments put forward by its author. In the course of leading the reader through what I consider to be some of the salient features of this dialogue I also pursue a line of interpretation of my own, which may be summarized as follows. In this book I argue that the view of the soul in the *Phaedo* can be usefully separated into two concepts; the first is what I have termed the *basic* concept, which consists of the features of the soul which are not used by the character Socrates as the basis for arguments showing either the pre-existence or post-existence of the soul; the second is what I have termed the *total* concept, which includes the features contained in the basic concept, plus all additional features that are used as the basis of arguments intending to prove either the pre-existence or the post existence of the soul, *plus* the features of pre-existence and post-existence themselves. My primary text is the *Phaedo* but, through the course of this study, I also look at the view of the soul presented by the character Socrates in four other Platonic dialogues. I do this as a means of clarifying the presentation in the *Phaedo* and contrasting it with some of the other significant presentations of the soul given within what are often considered Plato's early and middle dialogues.

I try to prove the usefulness of this interpretive method by illustrating the results of its application in the analysis of the view of the soul in the *Phaedo*. By using such a tool, and separating two concepts of the soul in the *Phaedo*, even where Plato has not explicitly done so, I argue that two further questions can also be answered. First, it clarifies some aspects of Plato's arguments for immortality (including the nature of these arguments, their relation to each other, and how the arguments for immortality in the *Phaedo* can begin to be contrasted to those given in other Platonic dialogues). And secondly, by using this interpretive method I am able to identify with some clarity the various features of the soul that emerge from an examination of the arguments within the dialogue.

I should like to say that it is my sincere desire that this modest work may give aid to the contemplation of that treasure about which Christ said that the wise among us would sacrifice all else to obtain.

Feast of St. Francis of Assisi
October 2006
Regent's Park College, Oxford

Abbreviations and References

ANCIENT AUTHORS AND WORKS

Hdt.	Herodotus
Hom.	Homer
Olymp.	Olympiodorus
Com.Phdo.	*Commentary on the* Phaedo
Pl.	Plato
Ap.	*Apology*
Euthy.	*Euthyphro*
Men.	*Meno*
Phdo.	*Phaedo*
Phdr.	*Phaedrus*
Rep.	*Republic*
Symp.	*Symposium*

MODERN WORKS AND EDITIONS

LSJ   Liddell, H.G., R. Scott and H. S. Jones, *A Revised Greek-English Lexicon*. Oxford: Clarendon Press, 1968.

JB   Burnet, John, edited with notes, *Plato's* Phaedo, Oxford: Clarendon Press, 1911.

LGW   Westerink, L.G. *The Greek Commentaries on Plato's Phaedo: Volume 1: Olympiodorus*. New York: North-Holland Publishing Co., 1976.

TMR   Robinson, T.M. *Plato's Psychology*, 2nd edition. Toronto: University of Toronto Press, 1995.

Chapter One

General Introduction

THE SCOPE OF THIS BOOK

Plato's *Phaedo* has attracted considerable attention since antiquity.[1] In this dialogue Plato provides us with a moving description of Socrates' last hours and final conversation with a group of his friends. We see, for example, Socrates calming the fears of timorous Cebes and his companion Simmias as they both, in their own way, prepare to lose their beloved in death. In the course of Socrates' soothing consolation he narrates his understanding of a number of important teachings, including an argument prohibiting suicide, the nature of philosophical calm in the presence of death, the value of purification or *katharsis*, and the nature of the human soul and its immortality.[2] The *Phaedo*'s primary influence upon the subsequent philosophical and theological traditions that developed within Europe and the Middle East has been through its presentation of the doctrine of the immortality of the individual human soul,[3] and it is to the study of the original Platonic formulation of this doctrine that we turn our attention.

While the pedagogical aim of this book is to introduce the reader to Plato's presentation of the soul in the *Phaedo*, the means by which I will do this is to lead the reader through the text with a methodological question in view: namely, *by what method can we best interpret Plato's presentation of the soul in the* Phaedo *as given through the character Socrates?* By separating the character Socrates' comments about the soul into a *basic* concept and a *total* concept I argue that we can better understand two other questions: first, what sorts of arguments for immortality does Socrates make in this dialogue? and second, what is the concept of the soul that emerges through the course of Socrates' argumentation and discussion about the soul? This exercise is one way to help us to go further into the text.

This being said I have limited this study in four ways.[4] First, I limit the study primarily to Plato's *Phaedo* and only look to other Platonic dialogues as they serve to illumine the teaching of this text. Second, I have restricted the scope of inquiry to the views held by the character Socrates; I concern myself only with what Plato has presented of the character Socrates' views through the argument and action of the dialogue.[5] By narrowing our study to Plato's presentation of the views of the character Socrates, we avoid the interesting but complex problem of determining the correct characterization of which are the opinions of the Socrates of history, and which are of the Socrates of Plato's literary invention. Next, it is important to distinguish between investigating his description of the individual human soul, and the character of its existence in the afterlife. In what follows, for the most part, I leave aside the separate question of Socrates' view of what happens in the underworld, and his ideas of the various punishments and rewards that await those who pass beyond bodily death.[6] Finally, I look at Plato's arguments about the soul's immortality, primarily with a view to understanding *the concept of the soul*. My main goal is to provide an articulate presentation without an evaluation of the philosophical cogency of his arguments.[7]

FOUR ASPECTS OF THE *CONCEPT* OF THE SOUL

As in all scientific investigations, before we turn to the texts it is important to know what to look out for. We should have some idea as to what kind of things might be said about the soul and, though allowing that these suggestions may later be contradicted, I suggest we keep a look-out for four lines of inquiry which would explore the soul's nature or essence; operations or activities; relation to the body; and any acquired habits or states that modify either of the other aspects. Although there may be more aspects of the human soul to consider, I do not believe there can be any less; and why this is so is not difficult to see.

To begin with, an account must be able to say something about what the soul is in itself. It must be able to describe something of the essence or *what-ness* of the thing we are trying to learn about. I suggest that this description should include a definition of the defining characteristic or characteristics apart from which a soul could no longer be thought to be a soul. And even if one has to concede ignorance of what that nature is after the end of the dialogue, having paid attention to what has been left unsaid by Plato will itself be of some benefit to our own thinking on the matter.[8] Further, a concept of the soul should also say something of the activities or operations carried out by the soul. In this we provide a description, not of what the soul is, but of what the soul does. Someone talking about the human soul should also give an account of its relation to the body. For whatever philosophical conclusion you come to about the status of the physical side to our existence one cannot but begin by noticing that which is most common in our notions: and what is most common is certainly that we do have a body! So in this third line of inquiry we answer how it is that the body and soul are distinguished, how it is that they affect each other, and whether they may be separable. Lastly, a concept of the soul should be able to speak about the states and habits that may modify the other aspects already mentioned. In Plato's terms, the most apparent examples of the acquired states of the soul are the virtues and vices. He argues that the soul's virtue or excellence effects how it can perform its activities. Throughout I will try to point out how Plato's account gives an answer to the above considerations.

TWO CONCEPTS OF THE Ψυχή IN THE *PHAEDO*

The thesis I argue for in this book is a relatively modest claim. The concept of the soul in the *Phaedo* can usefully be separated into two: the *basic* concept and the *total* concept. The *total* concept is the whole or complete concept of the soul presented by the character Socrates, while the *basic* is only a lesser part which I distinguish from the whole concept. The *basic* concept of the soul refers to features of the soul not used by the character Socrates as the basis for arguments showing either the pre-existence or the post-existence of the soul; the *total* concept of the soul refers to the concept that includes all features held within the *basic* concept, *plus* the additional features that Socrates will argue for within the *Phaedo* that he thinks provide the basis for arguments demonstrating its pre-existence and post-existence *and* the features of pre-existence and post-existence themselves. I do not suppose that the two concepts are something that I or anyone else might discover in the text itself, strictly speaking. Rather, is it an hermeneutical tool. Interpreting the text this way will help us to more thoughtfully engage in Plato's discussion of the immortal soul.

We might consider why this is an important argument to make at all. Drawing out the distinctions between the *basic* and the *total* concepts of the soul is a means of bringing to light the argumentation of the text. And, as I have already mentioned, this is one helpful way by which we can come to a better understanding of one of the central themes of the dialogue. Pointing out the distinctions between the *basic* concept (in which Socrates makes no assertions of the immortality of the soul) and the *total* concept (in which Socrates does assert the immortality of the soul) illuminates and helps us to identify the sort of arguments that Socrates is making before his friends. Along this line I will conclude that, although the goal of Socrates' arguments is to prove that the soul is immortal, the means by which he does this is by producing arguments about certain features of *an already existing soul*. This is the key to notice. As we shall see, nowhere in the *Phaedo* does Socrates give an argument for the *existence* of the soul, as such. That fact is a rather surprising element of the whole dialogue and offers a clue into what Socrates is about in the following pages. Socrates does not argue for the existence of an immortal soul, but for additional features to be added onto the concept of an already existing soul: he argues that the soul has certain features and that those features *entail* immortality.

Another benefit of this interpretive method follows from the first. After recognizing what sort of arguments Socrates is presenting, we will be in a better position to identify the *features of the soul* themselves that emerge through Socrates' arguments for immortality. These will be made clear in due time so there is no need to elaborate now.

Furthermore, this interpretive procedure provides a basis from which one is able to begin the work of comparing and contrasting arguments for immortality within the *Phaedo* to other Platonic dialogues, particularly those considered to be written in the 'middle' period.[9]

STRUCTURE OF THE BOOK

This present chapter serves as an introduction to the aims and methods particular to this book. In Chapters Two and Three I analyze Plato's concept of the soul in the *Phaedo*. Herein lies the heart of the argument. In Chapter Two I describe the *basic* concept of the soul in the *Phaedo*; in Chapter Three I examine the conception of the soul found within the *Phaedo* but this time taking note of the additional features (whether these pertain to the soul's nature, activities, relation to the body, or qualifying states) that Socrates presents as entailing, or providing the basis of arguments that show forth the soul's immortality, as well as the features of pre-existence and post-existence themselves. Having studied the concept of the soul in the *Phaedo*, in chapter Four I look at some alternative treatments of the soul and arguments for its immortality that are presented in four of Plato's dialogues (*Meno, Symposium, Republic,* and *Phaedrus*); these are usually considered to have been written near the same time and are thematically related to the *Phaedo*. These investigations provide the basis of the comparative work that I will do at the end of that chapter. By comparing and contrasting the various ways that Plato describes the nature of the soul, its activities, relation to the body, and acquired states, we will be able to appreciate something of the diversity, and possibly even the development, of Plato's view of the soul as he presents it through the character Socrates. In the last chapter I summarize and make explicit what I take to be the conclusions of the argument of this book. As a final word, I say what I take to be the moral value or intention of Socrates' arguments for immortality.

NOTES

1. Three such ancient commentaries that have survived to the present day is that by Olympiodorus (ca.495–565) and the two by Damascus (ca. 462–537). For a good discussion on the reception and influence of Plato's *Phaedo* in antiquity see *LGW* (pp.7–20) in the introduction to Westerink's English translation of Olympiodorus' commentary. Since the work of John Burnet (1863–1928) in the early part of the 20th century there have been numerous full-length studies and a host of scholarly papers devoted to the explication and interpretation of the *Phaedo*. For commentary on the influence of Burnet's work on the interpretation of Plato and Greek philosophy, as well as a listing of his writings see the memoir written by Lord Charnwood (3–22) in the collection of Burnet's essays, *Essays and Addresses*, (Freeport, New York: Books for Libraries Press, 1968). For a bibliography of commentaries and translations see David Bostock's *Plato's Phaedo*, (Oxford: Clarendon Press, 1986) and the bibliography given at the end of Martha C. Beck's recent commentary *Plato's Self-Corrective Development of the Concepts of Soul, Forms and Immortality in Three Arguments of the* Phaedo, (Lewiston, New York: The Edwin Mellen Press, Ltd., 1999).

2. There have been various ways of describing the themes of the dialogue. One of the earliest divisions is that given by Albinus, the second century Platonist, who in his commentary on the *Phaedo* divides the subject matter of the dialogue into three parts: the description of who the philosopher is (through the example of Socrates), the explanation of the aim of his life (detachment from the body), and a presentation of the fundamental supposition of Socrates' educational thought (the immortality of the soul). Cf. *LGW*, 10–11.

3. In relation to Plato's influence upon the development of patristic thought, Henry Chadwick's *Early Christian Thought and the Classical Tradition: Studies in Justin, Clement, and Origen* (Oxford: OUP, 1966) is a good general introduction and makes reference to Plato's doctrine of the immortal soul particularly in his chapter on Origen. Oscar Cullmann's well-known lecture *Immortality of the Soul or the Resurrection of the Dead? The Witness of the New Testament*, (London: The Epworth Press, 1958) is a modern criticism of the historical union of the philosophical doctrine of the immortal soul with the biblical doctrine of the resurrection. Cullman's study argues that the Pauline and Platonic doctrines of the nature of the soul are in fact incompatible. Jan N. Bremmer's, *The Rise and Fall of the Afterlife*, (London: Routledge, 2002), is a fairly accessible treatment of the idea of personal immortality and its influence upon the doctrinal development of the major monotheistic religions.

4. I refer the reader here to a number of important works that have dealt with Plato's view of the soul and the afterlife. John Burnet's treatment of the early Platonic doctrine of the soul in a lecture entitled *The Socratic Doctrine of the Soul* given at the Second Annual Philosophical Lecture: Henriette Hertz Trust, *Proceedings of the British Academy* 7 (1916): 235–259 was an influential work in this past century on the subject. T.M. Robinson's work, *Plato's Psychology*, second edition (Toronto: UTP, 1995) is a comprehensive study on Plato's doctrine of the soul, although it does not contain a thorough presentation of the various conceptions of the afterlife presented in the dialogues. There are a number of full-length studies in English devoted specifically to the *Phaedo* and its presentation of the doctrine of the immortal soul, of which I mention three. David Bostock's commentary *Plato's* Phaedo, (Oxford: Clarendon Press, 1986) is quite accessible; David Gallop's *Plato*: Phaedo, (Oxford: Clarendon Press, 1975) includes both a translation and a more detailed discussion that makes reference to the Greek text; Martha C. Beck's *Plato's Self-Corrective Development of the Concepts of Soul, Forms and Immortality in Three Arguments of the* Phaedo, (Lewiston, New York: The Edwin Mellen Press, Ltd., 1999) focuses almost exclusively upon the arguments for immortality themselves.

5. Those who wish to pursue further the question of the relation between the historical Socrates and the Socrates presented by Plato may begin by looking at three works. First, John Burnet gives a brief introductory discussion of the relation between the historical Socrates and Plato's Socrates in his work *Greek Philosophy: Thales to Plato*, (London: Macmillan and Co., Ltd., 1964), 102–122, and summarises his position, which I regard as judicious, as follows: "The conclusion we are, in my opinion, forced to is that, while it is quite impossible to regard the Sokrates of Aristophanes and the Sokrates of Xenophon as the same person, there is no difficulty in regarding both as distorted images of the Sokrates we know from Plato. The first is legitimately distorted for comic effect; the latter, not so legitimately, for apologetic reasons. To avoid misunderstanding, I should say that I do not regard the dialogues of Plato as records of actual conversations, though I think it probable that there are such embedded in them" (pp. 120–121). Next, one may turn to Gregory Vlastos' important work *Socrates: Ironist and Moral Philosopher*, (New York: Cornell University Press, 1991) where he develops the argument that there are a number of various and distinct "Socrates'" presented through Plato's writings. Vlastos claims that the opinions of the actual Socrates of history may be known, by the evidence of Plato and other ancient authors, in the dialogues of Plato's early period (cf. p.106). He says: "In different segments of Plato's corpus two philosophers bear that name [Socrates]. The individual remains the same. But in different sets of dialogues [Socrates] pursues philosophies so different that they could not have been depicted as cohabiting the same brain throughout unless it had been the brain of a schizophrenic. They are so diverse in content and method that they contrast as sharply with one another as with any third philosophy you care to mention, beginning with Aristotle's. This is a large claim. I shall be arguing for it in this chapter and the next" (p.46). Finally, for an accessible introduction to the problem of identifying the historical Socrates and for a bibliography of some of the important scholarly discussions on this topic written after Vlastos, see

Thomas C. Brickhouse and Nicholas D. Simth, *The Philosophy of Socrates*, (Boulder, Colorado: Westveiw Press, 2000), 33–52.

6. For a discussion of Socrates' views on death and the afterlife see the discussion in Thomas C. Brickhouse and Nicholas D. Smith's *Plato's Socrates*, (Oxford: OUP, 1994), 201–212.

7. There have been many discussions of the philosophical merit of Plato's arguments for immortality in the *Phaedo*. In Olympiodorus' 6th century Neoplatonic commentary on the *Phaedo* he points out that there existed a diversity of opinion among the leading philosophers at that time. For instance, Iamblichus considered each of the arguments for immortality in the dialogue to provide independent proofs. Olympiodorus' own view (and apparently that of the philosophical community at Alexandria) was that none of the arguments save the final one in the *Phaedo* prove the soul to be immortal (cf. *Com.Phdo.* Lecture 11, paragraph 2). Many 20th century commentators think that the proofs are inconclusive. However, there is divergence of opinion regarding whether or not Plato himself considered the arguments to be sound. For a summary of the views held within contemporary scholarship see Martha C. Beck's commentary wherein she provides an overview of the conclusions of Martha Nussbaum, Gregory Vlastos, David Bostock, Hans-Georg Gadamer and others upon this question. Cf. *ibid.*, 145–149.

8. I am aware that my description of what goes into an explanation of a "nature" or "essence" is brief and incomplete. What, exactly, satisfies as a description of an essence is a very difficult question and one which occupies, for example, much of Plato's *Meno*. By describing the nature as the characteristic feature by virtue of which a thing is what it is I believe I am following what appears to be the direction of the results of Socrates' explorations in the *Meno* (cf. *Men.* 72C; 73C-D; 75A-B). I will say more about this in Chapter Four.

9. I refer to the 'middle' dialogues merely as a convenient way of alerting the reader to various sets of dialogues that share certain features such as, in this case, certain common *thematic* features. For a summary of the conclusions and some of the arguments intended to establish the relative chronology of Plato's dialogues based on stylometric and other tests see David Ross', *Plato's Theory of Ideas*, (Oxford: Clarendon Press, 1961), 1–10. For arguments against the possibility and usefulness of determining the chronological sequence of the dialogues see Leo Strauss' *The City and Man*, (Chicago: University of Chicago Press, 1978), especially his chapter 'On Plato's *Republic*', and Leon Harold Craig's, *The War Lover: A Study of Plato's* Republic, (Toronto: UTP, 1996), 323.

Chapter Two

The *Basic* Concept of the ψυχή in the *Phaedo*

INTRODUCTION

The view of the soul held by Socrates within the *Apology* was uncontroversial to his listeners. In that dialogue Socrates offered little elaboration on, and no defense for, his understanding of the soul. What he was far more concerned with in the *Apology* was to convince the Athenians of the exceptional *value* of the soul, and to provide a reasoned justification for the (philosophical) way of life that followed from such a conception of the soul's value. In the *Phaedo* the situation is very different. We meet Socrates in his final hours of life. He is among his closest comrades, and the conversation turns to an extended discussion of the soul, the afterlife, and the implications these have on how a philosopher ought to live. Here the character Socrates *does* affirm a doctrine of the natural immortality of the individual human soul. The majority of the dialogue is a reported discussion between Socrates and his friends wherein Socrates labors to convince his companions that the soul will continue to exist after the body dies, and in fact will never cease to exist. He tries to persuade his friends of this by clarifying certain features that he believes belong to the soul and entail its undying nature. Later, in the next chapter, I will examine what those features are, and how Socrates uses them to argue for that immortality. The goal of this present chapter, however, is to explain the conception of the soul held by the character Socrates in the *Phaedo* in so far as this can be done without mentioning those features he believes imply the soul's immortality.

The first thing to keep in mind as we turn to the dialogue is that, like the Socrates of the *Apology*, the Socrates of the *Phaedo* speaks to his friends taking it for granted that some sort of soul exists, and that they ought to have no trouble believing this fact. For the purposes of later evaluation we do well first to single out the features of the soul that Socrates takes to be easily grasped, from those features that can be recognized only after long and sustained argument.

This chapter is divided into three parts. Below I outline the structure of the dialogue as a whole, following the main divisions of the text as I have outlined them. Then I analyze the *Phaedo* from the point of view of the *basic* concept of the soul. In this I draw attention to texts that reveal the conception of the soul's nature as, among other things, the locus of consciousness and moral habits; I provide additional information about the soul, but generally *exclude* those features that Socrates will identify as implying either the soul's pre-existence or post-existence. After that I summarize what I take Socrates' *basic* concept of the soul in the *Phaedo* to consist of.

DIVISION OF THE SUBJECT MATTER OF THE TEXT OF THE *PHAEDO*

I will refer to this outline at various points throughout the book, and I have placed in bold font those sections of the text that I pay special attention to in Chapter Three.

I. *Introduction to the whole dialogue* (57A-61C): Dramatic introduction and opening conversation between Phaedo and Echecrates wherein the setting and some of the themes of the dialogue are introduced.

II. *Main Body* of the whole dialogue (61C-115A): Socrates attempts to prove to his friends the reasons for his belief that a philosopher should face death with cheerfulness by showing that the soul is such that it is immortal; Socrates will attempt to show that the individual human soul retains both intelligence and capability after death; through the course of his arguments a number of features of the soul come to light.

II.A. *First Primary Section* of the main body (61C-69E): Socrates makes clear why he is cheerful in the face of death.
1. Socrates claims that killing oneself is not allowed since humans belong to the gods; this rule applies even to philosophers for whom death would bring great benefits.
2. Socrates defends the position that the philosopher will not fear death; to pursue wisdom requires the practice of purification (κάθαρσις) of the soul.

II.B. *Second Primary Section* of the main body (69E-80D): Three arguments to prove the soul to be immortal (ἀθάνατος).
1. **First argument: Generation from opposites (70C-72E).**
2. **Second argument: Learning as recollection (72E-77D).**

The Basic *Concept of the* ψυχή *in the* Phaedo 11

> *Brief Dramatic interlude: Socrates says that their desire for further argumentation is based upon childish fears; they should seek out an enchanter to help to rid them of their fear of death (77E-78B).*
> **3. Third argument: The soul has similarities to the Forms and to divinity (78B-80D).**

II.C. *Third Primary Section* of the main body (80D-84B): Socrates describes what happens after death to the immortal souls of various types of people; those who esteem injustice, those who lack virtue, those who have virtue but only through habit; as well, **The soul of the philosopher in the afterlife (80D-84B)** who has practiced purification (κάθαρσις) during life.

II.D. *Fourth Primary Section* of the main body (84C-107B): Cebes and Simmias raise objections to the arguments for immortality; Socrates offers a series of replies to these objections.
   1. Introduction: Socrates encourages Cebes and Simmias to express any doubts about the arguments.
   2. Main Body of the fourth primary section: Objections to the arguments for immortality and Socrates' replies to them.
      a. Objections (85B-88B)
         i). Objections made by Simmias: the body is related to the soul as a musical instrument is to its proper tuning; once the body (instrument) is destroyed, so is the soul (the resulting effect of the properly tuned instrument) also destroyed.
         ii). Objections made by Cebes: the body is to the soul as a cloak is to the tailor who made it; Cebes asks Socrates to show not only that the soul is immortal (ἀθάνατος), but also that it is everlasting (ἀνώλεθρος).
         Brief Dramatic interlude: the discussion is interrupted by Phaedo and Echecrates; Echecrates expresses uncertainty as to which arguments are to be believed, while Phaedo praises Socrates' skill as an educator even in his final hours of life (88C-89A).
      b. Replies by Socrates to the objections (89B-107A).
         i). Introduction: Socrates gives a warning against *misology*, the mistrust of argumentation; he begins his response by asking both if they agree that learning is recollecting and that the soul pre-exists the body.
         ii). Socrates replies to Simmias by refuting the view that the soul is a material harmony.
         iii). Socrates replies to Cebes by recounting his own intellectual biography. First, he recounts how he came to understand the

cause of generation and decay not through the method of natural philosophy but by an understanding of the Forms as the cause for why things are the way they are. Second, Socrates gives his **Fourth Argument: The soul as the principle of life will not admit its opposite (102B-106E)**, and for this reason is both immortal (ἀθάνατος) and everlasting (ἀνώλεθρος).

3. Conclusion to the Fourth Primary Section (107A-107B) in which both Cebes and Simmias agree with Socrates' position; Simmias admits to still having uneasiness about the arguments.

II.E. *Fifth Primary Section* of the main body (107C-115A): Socrates again speaks about what happens after death to the souls of various types of persons: to the incurably wicked, the curably wicked, those who have lived an average life, the extremely pious, and the philosophers.

III. *Closing Dramatic Scene* (115A-118A): Socrates makes preparations for his own death and is given the poison by the jailor; Socrates emphasizes the distinction between his real person, which they have been talking to, and the body which they will soon be burying; Socrates dies.

FEATURES OF THE ψυχή NOT USED AS THE BASIS FOR ARGUMENTS FOR IMMORTALITY

Introduction to the whole dialogue (57A-61C) and first primary section of the main body (61C-69E). We see in these sections a confirmation of much that was said about the soul in the *Apology*. The character Socrates holds the soul to be the locus of self-conscious rational thought. It is the soul that is responsible for rational inquiry, and it is the soul that is able to perceive reality. While separating out some of the differences between the activities of the body and of the soul, Socrates asks Simmias:

> Then what about the actual acquiring of knowledge? Is the body an obstacle when one associates with it in the search for knowledge. . . . Do you not think so? /I certainly do, he said. /When then, he asked, does the soul grasp the truth? For whenever it attempts to examine anything with the body, it is clearly deceived by it./True. /Is it not in reasoning if anywhere that reality becomes clear to the soul? 65A-C[1]

Socrates tells us something about the relationship between the soul and the body. Notice that he does this in four ways: by contrasting their methods of inquiry, their highest objects of inquiry, the degree of certainty their methods yield, and the objects desired by them which give them pleasure.

Socrates distinguishes the soul from the body (σῶμα) by means of their distinct methods through which they seek to grasp or perceive reality. The method by which the soul itself examines reality is through logical reasoning. The method by which the soul examines through the senses of the body is one of empirical observation. Here we have a straightforward, though rather unsophisticated, division of the methods of inquiry. But the soul is also distinct in relation to its object of highest inquiry. The soul seeks knowledge of intellectual and immaterial objects, such as the just (δίκαιον αὐτὸ), the beautiful, and the good (65D). Where the highest objects of attention of the ψυχή are intelligible, the highest objects the soul grasps through σῶμα are material.

This leads to a third, rather surprising, difference. He says, "men do not find any truth in sight or hearing" (65B). Quite obviously this is just the sort of mediation that we are naturally most accustomed to. However, for Socrates, the soul does not attain an accurate understanding of things when it examines reality through the body alone. In fact, the very idea is impossible, since judgment is always a necessary component to our perceptions. Without judgment we would have no way of organizing or interpreting what it is that the senses communicated. Viewed on their own, the senses invariably lead us to error. Most important is the fact that senses only provide mediation for sensible objects. Being physical themselves, they cannot perceive or mediate to the soul the essential or *unchanging* features of objects. Of course we may come to know something about the world through reflection upon what is given to us through the senses, but this something that we can understand through the mediation of the senses is not considered valuable to the philosopher. Knowledge of "what is most true in things" is gained only through grasping the forms, which by their very nature are intelligible, i.e. abstracted from matter (65DE).[2]

The last way in which Socrates contrasts the soul with the body is in the nature of the objects wherein each finds satisfaction. While the soul desires to grasp the truth, the body desires material and sensual pleasures such as food, sex, and the acquisition of fine clothing (64D). Socrates mentions that it is these desires within human beings that cause war (presumably because material goods are limited and tend to incite competition for resources) (66C).[3] He says that one way philosophers can be identified as a group is by the fact that they desire the truth even more than bodily pleasures (66E). The objects of desire for the philosopher are not the sort that change, but are permanent realities, and qualify as objects of knowledge (cf. 84A).

Second Primary Section of the main body (69E-80D). It is within the second primary section of the main body that we find three of Socrates' four arguments for immortality. Not surprisingly, little in Socrates' descriptions in this section contributes to our understanding of the *basic* concept. Between

69E-80D Socrates argues that the soul is a principle of life (71E), that it performs the activity of learning as recollecting (72E), and that it is invisible and similar to the forms (80A), all features of the soul which do not belong to the *basic* concept but which will be considered in the next chapter.

Third primary section of the main body (80D-84B). In this section Socrates turns to the theme of the after-life and describes what happens to souls of people after death. In his description, however, we also learn a good measure about what brings healing to the soul even in this life. And it is within this section that the theme of the "care of the soul" is revisited (on this point compare *Phdo*.82D and *Ap*.29DE), but here in fuller detail. His discussion of how to care for the soul begins with a few words on the relationship of the soul to the body by contrasting their objects of cognition. This time, however, Socrates includes a description of what he takes to be the moral, epistemological, and metaphysical consequences of his views on the relationship of the soul to the body. The soul of the philosopher that trains itself to be free from unnecessary bodily desires undergoes a process of purification and illumination;[4] the soul that remains attached to the physical becomes ignoble and eventually "nothing seems to exist for it but the physical" (81B).

Nothing exists for this kind of human but the physical. There is an ineluctable link between our moral lives and our ability to remain open to the whole of reality. The familiar distinctions we have grown accustomed to, as between private and public, beauty and goodness, really find no place in Plato's all-encompassing vision of the good life. Caring for the soul means keeping watch over the best part of ourselves. It means remaining alert and attentive to all that is real and escaping the merely transitory, false, and illusory with all the skill at our command. The stakes are high. The soul of the non-philosopher, through its constant association with the physical, not only becomes foolish in its incapacity to be enlightened but becomes transformed, apparently, even in its very nature:

> [This sort of soul] is no doubt permeated by the physical, which constant intercourse and association with the body, as well as considerable practice, has caused to become ingrained in it . . . this bodily element is heavy, ponderous, earthy and visible. Through it, such a soul has become heavy and is dragged back to the visible region in fear of the unseen and of Hades. 81CD

The soul itself takes on materiality. However much Socrates' language on this metaphysical point is figurative and how much literal,[5] the moral point is clear enough. The soul, figuratively speaking, takes on a material nature the more it *unnecessarily* associates with the desires of the body. Casting his comments in the religious terminology of the Orphics he says that those who serve the desires of the body and seek its pleasures, coming to believe that nothing save the material exists, become impure. Their nature is rightly called "material" because such people disregard the care proper or fitting to an immortal soul. Acting as though their soul's nature were merely material, and with only material desires to attend to, leads to disastrous moral consequences. And habitual servitude to the senses leads to such degrading moral vices as gluttony, violence, and drunkenness (81E). When the soul lacks an immaterial good to seek (which is less familiar) it will tend to pursue immediate and material goods (which are more familiar), and that without the benefit of a moderating principle.

Epistemological materialism has moral consequences for the soul. By materialism I mean the dogmatic belief that the human soul can have no knowledge of immaterial objects of cognition. It is as much a sentiment or a way of approaching reality as a propositional belief. Socrates argues that when "nothing seems to exist [for the soul] but for the physical"—so that the soul hates and fears and avoids the intelligible (81B)—disaster follows in the realm of daily life and in the field of practical moral action. In contrast, the philosopher seeks to know immaterial objects, and gradually gains separation (i.e. independence) from the body by the practice of purification or *katharis*. Purification is the true means to care for the soul. This is a theme we shall return to below.

Fourth primary section of the main body (84C-107B). In this section Cebes and Simmias raise objections to Socrates' arguments for immortality, and Socrates offers a series of replies to these objections. In the discussion that follows we learn nearly as much about what Socrates does not believe about the soul (e.g. that the soul cannot be a harmony resulting from material elements of the body [92A-95A]) as what he does believe about the soul. In his reply to Cebes, Socrates recounts how he came to hold the Forms as causes (100D) and gives a proof to show that the soul is not only immortal (ἀθάνατος) but also everlasting, or indestructible (ἀνώλεθρος) (106D).

The most interesting features about the soul in this section, in terms of the *basic* concept, are made known in Socrates' comments about misology and his role as educator. At one point the reported dialogue breaks off while Phaedo and Echecrates comment on the seemingly hopeless state of the argument thus far.[6] Echecrates relates how Socrates had earlier made such convincing proofs about the soul's immortality, only to have these countered by other arguments that were as convincing as the first. How do we decide which arguments are sound? (88D) Phaedo responds to Echecrates' observations with a moving tribute to Socrates. He praises his ability to understand the individual souls of his friends and to speak to them in a way suitable to their particular characters and dispositions:

> I have certainly often admired Socrates, Echecrates, but never more than on this occasion. That he had a reply was perhaps not strange. What I wondered at most in him was the pleasant, kind and admiring way he received the young men's argument, and how sharply he was aware of the effect the discussion had on us, and then how well he healed our distress and, as it were, recalled us from our flight and defeat and turned us around to join him in the examination of their argument. 88E-89A

We see here Socrates' skill as educator or what we might now call a spiritual director. As educator he is able to both heal their distress, and turn their attention back to the argument at hand. The healing and turning around of his friends' souls was done through both the words and actions of Socrates. It is worth considering how exactly he educates, and what this tells us about Socrates' view of the human soul.

Foremost, Socrates warns his friends not to be *misologues*—haters of rational discourse. As having one's own trust broken by a number of people can lead to a generalized mistrust of all people, so too can having one's trust in the truth of the conclusions of particular arguments lead to a generalized mistrust of all argumentation as such (90D). This experience says nothing about the trustworthiness of reasoning in its ability to make truth and knowledge of reality come clearer to the soul (cf. 90E). Rather, what it shows is the lack of skill. Socrates' advice is the following: take courage! Persevere in the desire for soundness! Love argumentation as a means to discover the truth—not for its ability to defeat others and win the approval of opponents (91A). Counseling such Socrates patiently returns to their objections and reviews what had been established (91Dff.).

Form and content match exquisitely in the patient example of Socrates the teacher. In this argumentation Socrates shows that the educator must appeal to the reasoning part of the soul. But in his example we see that the educator must appeal no less to that which is imitative: for the soul is a lover of images. The soul has a given propensity to replicate images of the good as viewed through the motions of others. Socrates speaks more about education through images in the fourth book of the *Republic*; for now we may conclude the following: the soul's dispositions, or acquired habits of moral action and feeling, are formed for good or ill by both the *instruction* and *example* of others.

In addition to Socrates' comments on misology and his example as educator, we find confirmation that the soul is the seat of the moral habits and dispositions. In the course of mounting an argument to show that the soul should not be thought of as a kind of bodily harmony, Socrates appeals to Simmias by asking:

> Come indeed, by Zeus, he said. One soul is said to have intelligence and excellence (νοῦν τε ἔχειν καί ἀρετήν) and to be noble, another to both have folly and wickedness and to be base. Are those things truly said? /They are rightly said. *93B-C*

Again I draw attention only to an obvious point. Socrates holds the soul to be the part of the human being that can be evaluated in *moral terms*. The soul is the locus of the moral habits and dispositions of a person and the health of these indicate the value of the soul under discussion.

Fifth primary section (107C-115A) and *Closing dramatic scene of the dialogue (115A-118A)*. In these sections Socrates speaks about what happens to the souls of various persons after death; as well, we find Plato's description of the final moments and death of Socrates by hemlock. The moral dimension of the human is underscored. Also, Socrates emphasizes that his real self, that is, his soul, will no longer be present within his body after he has died. It is the soul which animates and gives life to the body. For this reason his friends ought not to grieve at seeing his body either burned or buried (115E).

CONCLUSION: STATEMENT OF THE BASIC CONCEPT OF THE SOUL ψυχή

The goal of this chapter has been to describe the concept of the soul in the *Phaedo* from an examination of those texts where Socrates discusses aspects of the soul which he does not regard as entailing immortality. An important point to keep in mind is that, like the Socrates of the *Apology*, we have seen that the Socrates of the *Phaedo* speaks to his friends taking it for granted that some type of soul indeed exists. Whether the soul exists is not in question. This unproblematic concept of the soul is what we shall hereafter refer to as the *basic* concept of the soul, and may be described in the following way: the defining characteristic or what makes up the essence of the soul is that it is the agent or the self-conscious person; it performs the activities of thinking (perceiving), and desiring after the knowledge of immaterial objects of cognition; the soul is the locus of moral habits and dispositions; the soul is distinct from the body, and (while joined to the body) attains excellence by striving to avoid preoccupation with the desires of the body, or with objects of bodily cognition, as much as is humanly possible.

NOTES

1. In this chapter and subsequent chapters I rely for quotations of the *Phaedo* on G.M.A. Grube's translation. I shall make occasional amendments and translations of my own; these will be signified by italicizing the Stephanus number. All references to the Greek, unless otherwise noted, are from Burnet's text (*JB*).

2. A further reason the body is a cause of error is because its own maintenance (such as when it is sick) requires that the soul turn its attention away from intellectual objects of cognition towards the care of the body. And this leaves little time for contemplating the truth. A third reason is that the results of sense experience are incapable of being properly interpreted without a further judgment by the intellect to distinguish which are accurate from the inaccurate perceptions. This seems to be the point of Socrates' comments at 60B-C where he says, "What a strange thing that which men call pleasure seems to be, and how astonishing the relation it has with what is thought to be the opposite, namely, pain! A man cannot have both at the same time. Yet if he pursues and catches the one, he is almost always bound to catch the other also, like two creatures with one head."

3. Throughout the *Phaedo* the cause of conflict within and among human beings is not due to a faulty ordering between the *parts* of the soul, as in the *Republic*, but because of the disordered relationship between the *soul* and the *body*.

4. By purification I am referring to the limiting of unnecessary desire and the education of the moral habits of a person. Illumination is what results from the method of purification, which I will discuss in greater detail in the next chapter.

5. Both the epistemological and moral consequences are more clearly presented than the metaphysical consequences. It seems that the materiality of the soul and its becoming "heavy, ponderous, earthly and visible" (81C) would be meant as an image, given Socrates' prior descriptions of the invisibility of the soul at 78Bff. However, the fact that Socrates then goes on to use his description of the 'material soul' as a basis for accounting for reported sightings of ghosts (81D) might temper our willingness to interpret his comments as being wholly figurative language. Hackforth takes the 'spatialist' language about the soul as purely metaphorical, whereas Robinson assigns more weight to such texts and argues that "all the metaphorical language is remarkable for its internal consistency and coherence, and I suggest a particular view of the soul, if only an unconscious one, underlines it. For the sake of a word, we may call it 'ectoplasm theory.'" Cf. *TMR*, 31. For my part, I agree with Hackforth in arguing that we should take Socrates' materialist references to the soul as metaphorical. The reason for this is that taking Socrates literally at this point would go against the vast majority of Socrates' other statements about the *immateriality* of the soul.

6. Burnet conjectures that the significance of this break in the reported dialogue form is that it returns us to our original characters and setting of the dialogue. Plato uses this dramatic interlude to show us that the "current Pythagorean views about the soul are inadequate and that we must go deeper" *JB*, note 88C1.

Chapter Three

The Concept of the ψυχή in the *Phaedo*: Features in Addition to the *Basic* Concept

INTRODUCTION

Near the opening of the dialogue Socrates makes a pair of puzzling claims. On the one hand Socrates contends that a true or genuine philosopher would be better off dead; on the other hand that a philosopher should not commit suicide. To justify the first claim Socrates defends the view that philosophy is the "practice of death and dying." Socrates' initial arguments are criticised by his friends Simmias and Cebes, and all those gathered playfully agree that Socrates should stand trial again to make a defence of his position. Socrates agrees to the challenge. He concedes, in fact, that the arguments intending to show how a philosopher ought to look forward to death might not make sense *but for the fact* that he expects to find himself in the future company of the gods. He says:

> I want to make my argument before you, my judges, as to why I think that a man who has truly spent his life in philosophy is probably right to be of good cheer (θαρρεῖν) in the face of death and to be very hopeful (εὔελπις εἶναι) that after death he will attain the greatest blessings yonder. I will try to tell you, Simmias and Cebes, how this may be so. I am afraid that other people do not realise that the one aim of those who practice philosophy in the proper manner is to practice for death and dying. 63E-64A

It is this conflict of claims, over whether a philosopher ought to be willing to die, that generates the action and the arguments presented in the dialogue for the immortality of the soul.

The goal of this chapter is to uncover the features of the soul that are in addition to the *basic* concept of the soul that we earlier saw within the *Phaedo* (a concept very similar to the complete concept of the soul in the *Apology*). These additional features that I point out in this chapter are made up of two groups: first, those additional features (whether of the soul's nature, activities, relation to the body, or acquired habits) that Socrates uses as the basis for proving that the soul is pre-existent and post-existent and, second, the features of pre-existence and post-existence themselves.

There are three principal ways by which Socrates reveals these additional features: through the various arguments for personal immortality, by his descriptions of the after-life, and in his recommendations of how a philosopher is to live in this present life. Accordingly, I have organised my comments into three parts. First, I look to see what features of the soul emerge during the course of Socrates' explicit arguments intending to show the human soul is immortal. This first part has four sections wherein I look at each of the main arguments for immortality (including indestructibility). In part two I look at the way that the soul, especially the soul of the philosopher, is presented in Socrates' descriptions of the afterlife. In the third part I look at how some of the features of the soul are made even more explicit through Socrates' teaching on how a philosopher ought to live his life on the earth; in particular, I look at Socrates' notion of *katharsis* as a necessary part of philosophical method in the soul's deliverance from the body and its passions. Here we will see that Socrates' view of the soul in the afterlife has a direct bearing on the way a philosopher lives on earth. Finally, I offer a statement on the complete notion of the soul held by Socrates within the *Phaedo*.

FOUR ARGUMENTS INTENDED TO PROVE THE ψυχή WILL SURVIVE DEATH AND EXIST FOREVER

Below I look at four separate arguments that Socrates offers as proofs for the immortality of the soul (that is to say, the fact that it will not only survive death but will exist forever): his arguments that generation occurs from opposites, that learning is recollection, that the soul has greater similarities to the Forms than to bodies, and his argument that the soul will not admit its opposite and is indestructible.

Before beginning the first proof Socrates explicitly states to his friends what he is aiming to achieve in all four of the arguments. He agrees with Cebes by affirming that he wants to show not only that the individual soul will forever survive bodily death, but also that it still "holds some capability and wisdom (τινα δύναμιν ἔχει καὶ φρόνησιν)" (*70B*). As we shall see, Socrates aims to show that the sort of soul he thinks will survive death forever is the same distinct person that animated the body during earthly life.¹ I am looking at each of these arguments not primarily from the point of view of evaluating them (i.e., not to see whether their premises are true, or whether those premises do in fact entail immortality), but rather as a means of understanding the concepts and arguments of Socrates' view of the soul. I am looking to see how he understands the four aspects of the soul mentioned earlier: the nature, activity, relation of the soul to the body, and any modifying states that the soul can acquire. In the following secitions, my analysis of Socrates' arguments proceeds by two stages. I outline the basic steps of the argument itself, and after that make explicit the features themselves.

1st ARGUMENT: GENERATION FROM OPPOSITES (70C-72E)

The argument about the nature of the generation of things from their opposites constitutes Socrates' initial attempt to prove that the soul will be able to survive the death of the body. Not far into the dialogue Socrates modifies this argument by joining it to the second, which is about learning and recollecting (77C). Nevertheless, even in this first attempt something of Socrates' view of the soul is made manifest, and so the argument has value for our study.

Socrates begins by recalling an ancient theory (παλαιὸς...λόγος) that states the living come from the dead and that souls arrive on earth from the dead (70C).² The remainder of the argument is given as a hypothetical explanation of the consequences that must follow from this ancient theory. The most obvious consequence is that souls must have existed in Hades, the underworld and the place of the dead. The theory is convincing, however, because of more than its ancient origin. He goes on to suggest that if his friends consider not only human beings, but also the generation of plants and animals and everything that comes into existence, they could better grasp the principle upon which the theory depends. He proposes that whatever comes into existence comes to be from its opposite, if it has one. Examples of opposites are such pairs as the beautiful and the ugly, and the just and the unjust (70E).

Socrates suggests that there are two principles at work between any pair of opposites in the process of generation. From the first member of the pair comes the second member of the pair, and then again from the second comes the first. That is, in any pair of opposites that come into existence, A leads to B, and B leads back to A (71B). Socrates gives an example of these principles at work in the movement between life and death. At the close of his reflections on this two-fold process of generation Socrates feels confident to ask

Cebes: "Then, Cebes, living creatures and things come to be from the dead?" Cebes affirms this, and Socrates concludes, "Then our souls exist in the underworld" (71E). Socrates adds by way of clarification that if there is such a thing as coming to life again it would be a process of coming to life *from the dead*. Thus, as living leads to dying, so the process of dying eventually causes its opposite within the pair to be generated. Things come to life from the dead, and become dead from being alive. If this were not so then an absurd conclusion would follow. If things did not return to their opposite form (as a living thing eventually becomes a dead thing and vice versa), everything would at some point stop at one form and there would cease to be any generation at all: everything would at some moment become dead (72D). Since not everything has been absorbed in death, however, we can have some confidence that a process of generation through opposites does in fact occur. For Socrates, as for Aristotle, there is no creation *ex nihilo*.

There is a good deal lacking within this argument. We have already noted that Socrates admits as much within the course of this dialogue. Nevertheless, what can we understand of Socrates' view of the soul from this theory and the reasons he offers in support of it? At the outset it appears that the soul is identified with a principle of life. The soul is a principle of life in the sense that it is the cause of the life or animation of the physical body. This seems to me the case since the soul is associated with what is "living" in his explanation of the two-fold movement between dying and becoming alive. That the soul is "living" has important consequences; these will only be made more articulate further in the dialogue.

I think confusion at this point arises from the fact that Socrates does not specify what are the relevant opposing characteristics within his pairs. For instance, he represents life as the opposite to death (71E); Cebes agrees that it is by the generative process that the living comes from the dead. Yet oddly enough Socrates infers from this that "the souls of the dead must be somewhere whence they can come back again" (72A). If the soul is said to exist for the living as for the dead, in what function or capacity does the soul of a dead man operate at all? That is, if the soul of the dead man retains waking consciousness then in what way are we to consider him dead? Moreover, if the soul of the dead man really is *dead* then Socrates' argument, at least on the surface of things, is not achieving what it sets out to prove: that the soul lives on past death and in fact is immortal. Despite the imprecision of Socrates' way of speaking about the soul in this initial argument, I think we can take away from it the fact that Socrates holds the soul to be, in some manner, a principle of life. This principle will be expanded upon later in Socrates' fourth argument for immortality.

2nd ARGUMENT: LEARNING AS RECOLLECTION (72E-77D)

We turn next to Socrates' argument that what is commonly called learning is actually recollection (ἀνάμνησις). Following the conclusion of the first argument (with which Cebes seems to be wholly satisfied), in a touch of dramatic humour Simmias says he has forgotten that 'other proof' about the soul that Socrates is accustomed to mentioning. That 'other proof' is the argument that whenever we learn we are actually only recollecting knowledge that we had previously gained. Cebes remembers the main idea of the 'other proof' (in which the soul was also likely to be immortal) and at Simmias' request Socrates furnishes another—second—explanation of an argument that learning is actually recollecting. The basic idea is that we must have at some previous time learned what we now recollect. Recollection is possible, says Socrates, *only if* our souls existed somewhere before they took on human shape. Thus, since we *are* able to recollect knowledge, according to this current presentation of the theory of ἀνάμνησις, the soul is likely to be something immortal (73A). In his explanation of ἀνάμνησις (unlike that given in the *Meno*) Socrates discloses that the theory of learning as recollection of previously acquired knowledge is actually based upon the truth of a different theory altogether.

In the *Phaedo* the theory of learning as recollection is based upon a theory of the transcendent Forms. Through the course of his discussion Socrates provides a brief description of his doctrine of the ideal Forms and shows why it is the logically prior theory upon which the theory of recollection depends.[3] Socrates leads Simmias to agree that people possess knowledge of the concept of Equal itself prior to any time that they perceived objects of equal proportions through the senses. Socrates reasons:

> Then before we began to see or hear or otherwise perceive, we must have possessed knowledge of the Equal itself (αὐτοῦ τοῦ ἴσου ὅτι ἔστιν) if we were about to refer our sense perceptions of equal objects to it, and realised that all of these were eager to be like it, but were inferior. 75B

Continuing on a little further, Socrates says that we must also have possessed this knowledge of the Equal before we were born because the ability to see and hear is present from the very moment of birth.

> Therefore, if we had this knowledge, we know before birth and immediately after not only the Equal (τὸ ἴσον), but the Greater (τὸ μεῖζον) and the Smaller (τὸ ἔλαττον) and all such things, for our present argument is no more about the Equal than about the Beautiful itself, the Good itself, the Just, the Pious and,

as I say, about all those things to which we can attach the word "itself," ("αὐτὸ ὅ ἔστιν"[4]) both when we are putting questions and answering them. So we must have acquired knowledge of them all before we were born. 75CD

Whenever we recollect one object at the time of perceiving something similar (or dissimilar) to it, we are recollecting one of a certain class of objects that exists independently of sense perception. We refer all that we perceive to permanent, unchanging, and transcendent realities. Socrates concludes this line of argumentation by saying that since our ability to perceive inequalities among sensory objects is derived from knowledge of the Equal itself, it must be the case that our souls gained knowledge of the Forms before we had physical sense-perception. (He evidently does not consider it possible for knowledge of the Forms to be transmitted at the moment birth.) And so, as surely as those permanent realities exist, then so too must our souls have pre-existed our bodies so as to have been able to attain knowledge of them before birth (76E).

At the end of his discussion of learning Socrates recognises that this proof on its own is insufficient too. The theory of recollection can prove that the personal soul (as the Forms) existed *before* bodily life; however, it cannot itself show that the soul will continue to exist *after* death. At this point in his argument Socrates joins the second argument about the nature of learning and recollection to the first proof about the processes of generation. While the latter argument shows the soul must pre-exist, the former is needed to show that the soul will continue to exist even after the body has died.

What features of the soul are present in this second argument? The first is that Socrates explicitly names the soul as the part of the human being that has both memory and intelligence, and carries out the activities of learning. And it is through the soul that formerly acquired knowledge is brought into consciousness by giving aid to the memory. It is also through the soul that a person is able to reason and grasp the intelligible Forms. These features of learning (memory and intelligence) do not in and of themselves add significantly to the basic concept already argued for in the last chapter, but Socrates' treatment of them here is more extensive.

The implicit logical relation between memory, knowledge, and the permanence of the soul is now made explicit. Furthermore, the soul has also been shown, within this second argument, to have a certain resemblance to the ideal Forms themselves. He argues that since all bodily perception is logically dependant upon the knowledge of the Forms, and the Forms are non-bodily, it seems to follow that the soul gained its knowledge of the Forms (an event of which it now has no conscious memory) in a pre-bodily condition.[5] The relation between the nature of the Forms and the soul will be exploited further in the sequence of the next argument.[6]

3rd ARGUMENT: THE ψυχή IS SIMILAR TO THE FORMS AND TO DIVINITY (78B-80D)

We turn now to Socrates' third argument. In this the soul is shown to be immortal by virtue of the fact that its nature shares a greater likeness to the Forms than to the body, and that it shares a likeness to divinity. We look first at how Socrates presents the soul's affinity to the Forms.

It is interesting to note that, throughout the course of Socrates' explanation to Simmias and Cebes, his friends have not brought up any logical difficulties with the two arguments earlier presented. Rather, what prompts this next proof is his friends' confession to a childish fear. Simmias and Cebes admit that, despite the preceding arguments, they are arrested by the worry that their souls may scatter at death. Socrates tells them that the way to get rid of this sort of (irrational) fear is to sing a charm. "You should search for such a charmer among them all, sparing neither trouble nor expense, for there is nothing on which you could spend your money to greater advantage" (78A). After this dramatic interlude Socrates agrees to go on with the discussion and proceeds to the third argument.[7] He prefaces this argument by stating that they will together consider two questions: what kind of thing is likely to scatter? And what class of things does the soul belong to? Answering these two questions will enable his friends to know whether it is or is not reasonable to have confidence in the immortality of the soul in the face of death (78B).

What kind of thing is likely to scatter? Socrates conjectures that two classes of objects exist: composite and those that are not (78C). He details the various ways that these two types of things are spoken of. The composite is compound, liable to split up into component parts, and varies from one time to another. Composite things are particulars. On the other hand, the non-composite does not split up, and always stays the same. Further, the two types of objects are distinguishable not only by reference to their internal make-up, but in the manner by which they are grasped by humans. While the former are perceived by the physical senses, the latter are known only by the soul through thought (78E-79A).[8] Continuing on, Socrates adds that the human is a composite being. He gets Cebes to agree that "one part of ourselves is the body, another part is the soul" (79B).[9] In short, there are two types of existing things that make up the world, and two parts that make up a human being: composite objects are perceived by sense and likely to scatter, whereas non-composite things are neither perceived by sense nor likely to scatter.

Socrates turns to the second question and asks what class of thing the soul belongs to (79B). He answers, of course, that the soul belongs to the second sort of things, and the body to the first. In Socrates' answer we are able to determine additional features of the soul. In its nature, the soul is more akin to the invisible things; in its nature, the body is more like the visible.

Because the nature of the soul has some features that make it more like the Forms than like corporeal objects, Socrates thinks that the soul should also be described as having all of the features listed below:

> Consider then, Cebes, whether it follows from all that has been said that the soul is most like the divine, deathless, intelligible, uniform, indissoluble, always the same as itself, whereas the body is most like that which is human, mortal, multiform, unintelligible, soluble and never consistently the same. . . . Well then, that being so, is it not natural for the body to dissolve easily and for the soul to be altogether indissoluble, or nearly so? 80AB

Socrates' conclusions require further explanation in addition to what has so far been given, in order to draw out the precise nature of the argument for the soul's immortality that he is making.

Although there appears to be a measure of incompleteness in Socrates' explanation, I believe that the basic organization of his comments is given in terms of an argument from analogy. The Forms have one set of features, which includes immortality, and the soul has some of the same features as the Forms: therefore, by analogy, he thinks it likely that the soul has certain *other* features as the Forms too—most importantly, immortality. From the fact that the Forms are non-changing (ἀεὶ ἔχει) (78D) they should also be thought of as uniform or simple (αὐτὸ καθ' αὑτὸ) (cf. 78D), intelligible (i.e. graspable only by the reasoning power of the mind) (79A), and immortal (ἀθάνατος).[10] From the fact that the Forms are intelligible he also says they must be invisible (ἀιδῆ) (cf. 79A).

But which of the above features of the Forms does the soul have that, by analogy, also imply the immortality of the soul? We recall that Socrates had posited two classes of existence, and that the soul was said to be more like the invisible than the visible. And further, that the soul was concluded to be without parts or simple, as compared to the body which is made up of parts and is composite. Later on in the passage, at 79E, he appears to simply *assert* that the soul is more like that which is "always existing", that is, that which is immortal. But if we are to charitably interpret Socrates' discussion between 78B-80D we might be able to recognize the way he arrives at this conclusion. As I have said, he thinks that the Forms have the feature of being non-changing and they are also simple, intelligible, invisible, and immortal. Socrates' argument by analogy is that because the soul has the same features of being simple and invisible, it would also be likely to have the feature of immortality. *Since* the soul also has the features of being non-changing and invisible, *then* it should also have the other features of the Forms listed (such as being simple and intelligible) and, most importantly, the feature of immortality.

Socrates goes further than this, however, to claim for the soul some features that the Forms do not have. The soul shares an affinity not only with the Forms but also with the divine. On the basis of this affinity Socrates takes it as likely that the soul is something immortal. As the divine rules what is over the mortal (and lives forever), so also the soul rules over the body. Thus, as the divine rules and is immortal, so the soul is likely immortal since it also rules (80A). Socrates never presents his case here as more than a probabilistic argument.

4th ARGUMENT: THE ψυχή AS THE PRINCIPLE OF LIFE WILL NOT ADMIT ITS OPPOSITE (102B-106E)

We now come to the final argument for immortality.[11] Immediately preceding Socrates' fourth argument comes a lengthy discussion about the nature of cause, and the nature of the Forms as agents of causality. This discussion finds its place within Socrates' own account of his intellectual biography that he gives to Cebes to help strengthen his belief in the soul's undying nature. I will review a number of the main points covered in this previous section (96A-102A) because they are assumed within the formal argument that begins at 102B.

In the course of Socrates' intellectual biography he is concerned foremost with outlining how his views of the nature of causality developed. He began his intellectual inquiry by searching for the cause of generation and decay, and this by means of the methods of study used within the physical or natural science of his day (96A). One of the prominent thinkers he encountered in this exploration was the philosopher Anaxagoras. The philosopher had said that Mind (νοῦς)[12] directs and causes everything (97C). However, when Socrates looked more closely into how Anaxagoras explained things, he found that the philosopher actually made no use of Mind "nor gave it any responsibility for the management of things, but mentioned as causes air and ether and water and many other strange things" (98BC). Clearly, this sort of explanation would not do. Anaxagoras' view was lacking because it offered a series of material causes to account for all sorts of effects that Socrates believed could only be understood in terms of teleological or *purposeful ends*. For instance, Socrates found it ridiculous to give a detailed account of the workings of the bones and sinews of the human body to explain human action (99A).[13] While providing an account of how bones and sinew may interact with each other is one aspect of an explanation, it is useless if you want to know *why* people act as they do (98D)! To understand that, one must take into account the end or goal of the intended action. Socrates' chief criticism of Anaxagoras' view, therefore, is not so much that it is false, but that it is incomplete—and in this I think Socrates is entirely correct:

> To call bones and sinews causes is too absurd. If someone said that without bones and sinews and all such things, I should not be able to do what I decided, he would be right, but surely to say that they are the cause of what I do, and not that I have chosen the best course, even though I act with my mind (νοῦς) is to speak very lazily and carelessly. Imagine not being able to distinguish the real cause from that without which the cause would not be able to act as a cause. It is what the majority of people appear to do . . . 99AB

In place of Anaxagoras' material causes Socrates relates how he eventually came to believe in the Forms as causes, and particularly the Beautiful and the Good (100B). Socrates came to postulate that the *real* reason why things can be beautiful is because the Beautiful itself caused them to be such (100C). How it is that the Beautiful itself acts as a cause Socrates says very little; he will explore this in the *Republic*.

The beginning of this fourth argument thus starts off with Cebes having agreed to two things. First, that each of the Forms actually exists and, second, that the Forms act as a sort of cause (102B).[14] The argument that we will turn to below, that the soul will not admit what Socrates takes to be its opposite (death) and so must be able to live continuously, begins by assuming this theory of the transcendent Forms as agents of causation.

The proof begins with a reflection on the nature of the Forms. It is concluded that some Forms have opposing correlates. For instance, he takes Tallness and Shortness, and the Forms Odd and Even to be opposites. In both examples neither Form can become like or ever admit its opposite Form.

At this point in the argument, however, Phaedo breaks into his telling of the account of Socrates' final conversation and interjects how someone present at the discussion asked how this supposition could be reconciled with an earlier comment that was already agreed to. This interruption provides a most welcome opportunity in the dialogue for clarification. Phaedo relates to Echecrates how an unnamed participant reminded the group that it had been earlier accepted, in the course of the first argument for immortality, that things having an opposite were generated from their opposites and thus that the larger came from the smaller and vice versa (103A). The earlier view seems irreconcilable with the latter idea that an opposite will never admit an opposite. He says Socrates replied to the questioner in the following manner:

> You have bravely reminded us, but you do not understand the difference between what is said now and what was said then, which was that an opposite

thing came from an opposite thing; now we say that the opposite itself could never become opposite to itself, neither that in us nor that in nature. 103AB

But Socrates explains: then he was talking about things that have opposite qualities; now that these opposites themselves "from the presence of which in them things get their name" (i.e. the Forms) can never admit their own opposite (103B). But what exactly does this mean? To clarify, Socrates has Cebes agree to a set of relations that are opposing by admitting that as hot is distinct from fire, so also cold is distinct from snow (103D). Taking the opposite relations just mentioned, it is inconceivable that there could be such a thing as "hot-snow" or "cold-fire". Certain properties only arise out of certain substances or relations. As these opposites could not exist at the same time within one object, for the same reason it would be nonsense to suppose that there could be a "dead-soul"—since whatever soul occupies is made alive.[15]

But what is it that coming into the material body makes it a *living* body? (105C) Cebes, answering correctly, replies that it is the soul. Socrates claims that not only a human body, but whatsoever a soul occupies comes to life. This is an important point to keep in mind—because he takes the argument further by saying that the *opposite of life is death*. The result: since life always accompanies soul *and* death is the opposite of life, therefore, soul can never admit death.

Another question: how is it that the human soul, while in itself not a Form nevertheless acts like a Form in not admitting what is opposite to itself? Socrates' reply: while the soul is not a Form itself, it always has the Form life inhering within it. "Whatever the soul occupies, it always brings life to it" (105D). Where the soul is there life is also. He gives examples of other Forms which operate on a similar principle to help us understand how soul and death can never occupy the same place or time. Other Forms (as the uneven, unmusical, unjust) do not admit their opposite Forms (even, musical, just) (105D). In short, because the Form life always accompanies the soul, the soul would also share the property of not admitting the Form opposite to life *where and when soul is present*.

From the fact that the soul will not admit death, Socrates concludes that the soul is also immortal (ἀθάνατος). For the purposes of clarification and in response to Cebes' objection made at 87D-88B, Socrates temporarily restricts the meaning of the term 'ἀθάνατος' to that which merely lasts beyond bodily death. He then elaborates exactly what sort of immortality the above argument implies. Because the soul will not admit death, Socrates also thinks the soul is something that is not even able to be destroyed[16] (ἀδύνατον...ἀπόλλυσθαι) (106B). The soul not being able to be destroyed, in turn, means that the soul is also something everlasting or does not perish[17] (ἀνώλεθρος), capable not only of existing over a long period of time but indefinitely. To say this in another way, the soul that is immortal (ἀθάνατος) is not capable of being destroyed; *because* it is not able to be destroyed it is also everlasting (ἀνώλεθρος). Socrates temporarily limited the meaning of 'ἀθάνατος' only to return to it again the fuller sense of the term which now explicitly includes the concept of being something that never ceases to exist.

From the above, what more can we know about Socrates' view of the soul? In sum: the soul is a principle of life ("whatever the soul occupies, it always brings life"); and the soul lasts forever (the soul that is ἀθάνατος is also ἀνώλεθρος).

THE ψυχή OF THE GENUINE PHILOSOPHER IN THE AFTERLIFE (80D-84B; 114C-E)

In the next two parts of this chapter we leave behind Socrates' explicit arguments intending to prove the soul's immortality. In what follows we will consider how Socrates' view of the soul is made known within texts that deal with the moral character or habits and dispositions of the soul of the philosopher in the after-life.

At two places Socrates discusses the soul of the philosopher in the afterlife. The first comes immediately after Socrates' third proof of immortality and begins at 80D. We recall how the soul is more similar to the immaterial Forms than to the body. Moreover, Socrates posited that a human is a composite being having body and soul. Following this, Socrates describes the goal of philosophy and distinguishes the soul of the philosopher from the soul of the non-philosopher (80D-84B). (Most strikingly in this text, the practice of philosophy is characterized as training for death [81A], an idea that will be explored further in the next section.)

Between 80D and 84B Socrates describes what the after-life will be like for the philosopher. Having sought after deliverance in earthly life, the soul of the philosopher eventually finds itself in a disembodied state:

> A soul in this state makes its way to the invisible, which is like itself, the divine and immortal and wise, and arriving there it can be happy (εὐδαίμονι εἶναι), having rid itself of confusion, ignorance, fear, violent desires and the other human ills and, as is said of the initiates, truly spend the rest of time with the gods. 81A

The nature of the soul of the philosopher is invisible and divine-like. After death it has no more association with the corporeal; the soul is immeasurably happy. This comes about in two ways. It is happy by virtue of the character of the fellowship which it is now able to keep—being, as it is, in the midst of the gods (82B). (Presumably the soul is also able to keep company with other philosophers as well, but this, curiously, is nowhere stated.[18]) It is happy by virtue of its unceasing contemplation: the soul can now fix its gaze upon what is true and divine and not the object of opinion (84A). The philosopher before death is characterized by his longing to attain knowledge. And, with respect to the acquisition of knowledge and the activity of learning, what could only be approximated in life is fully achieved after death.

Between 114C-114E we find Socrates' second description of the soul of the philosopher after death. This comes at the end of Socrates' presentation of the Myth of the underworld. In the Myth Socrates describes the fate of four classes of people who receive four kinds of judgements; each will face a judgement and each be rewarded and punished according to their deeds done in the body (113Dff). Those who lived a decent but unremarkable life go into the Acheron River in the underworld; the incurably wicked are hurled into the Tartarus River for everlasting punishment; the curable wicked also go to the Tartarus River though for a shorter duration. From among the many human beings, it is the extremely pious and the philosophers who are singled out and receive exceptional rewards. Escaping the monotony of the underworld, the pious are released to the upper world (114C). The philosophers alone, however, are freed from corporeality. Those who have purified themselves through philosophy "live in the future altogether without a body; they make their way to even more beautiful dwelling places which it is hard to describe clearly . . ." (114C).[19]

Let me draw attention to three features given in the above texts. To begin with, Socrates affirms that the soul is the seat of the conscious personality, and that which provides for the capacity for rational thought. This aspect has been pointed to in Socrates' claim that a chief activity of the soul of the philosopher after death will be the contemplation of permanent realities (84A). After death the philosopher will have clear intellectual vision of the Forms. Thought continues. Secondly, we are given further insight into how Socrates thinks the body and soul relate to each other. At one point Socrates explained that a difference between the soul of a philosopher and a non-philosopher is that the former is entirely freed from the body after death, while the latter is not. In fact, Socrates went so far as to say that apparitions near graves and other burial monuments can be accounted for as the appearances of souls of the dead who have not been fully freed from corporeality (81C). It is because the souls of these persons had not been purified and cleansed from material desires that we are still able to see them—as shades—with our physical eyes. Third, it is again quite clear that in Socrates' view the soul is capable of attaining virtue, is capable of development. This aspect of Socrates' *total* concept of the soul has already been mentioned but receives additional clarification here. Through his description of the soul in the afterlife we come across an elaborate catalogue of states and acquired habits that modify the activities done through the soul. The virtues of moderation, bravery, righteousness, freedom, and truth are each listed as kinds of excellences that are the adornments of the soul which modify how it carries out its operations (114E). Moreover, the fact that virtue and the soul's separation from the body lead to happiness is perhaps more definitely emphasised here than in other part of the dialogue that we have looked at (81A). Happiness is the resulting by-product of virtue.

HOW THE TRUE PHILOSOPHER LIVES IN THIS LIFE: PHILOSOPHY IS THE TRAINING FOR DEATH

As we have seen above, the ultimate goal of the philosopher is achieved only after death and this in two ways. The philosopher will be happy after death because he wins fellowship with the gods and enduring contemplation of unchanging Forms. But given the goal of the soul of the philosopher we now ask: how is the philosopher to live in this life?

Above all else, the philosopher must pay attention to care for the welfare of his soul (μέλει τῆς ἑαυτῶν ψυχῆς) (82D). This theme was prominent in Socrates' exhortations in the *Apology* and we see that it also finds a significant place in this dialogue. In the *Phaedo* caring for the soul essentially means that all of the philosopher's actions are determined in light of the final goal for which he longs. This goal is the attainment of happiness (εὐδαίμων) (81A). The soul that avoids association with the body (80E, 81B) by withdrawing to itself and seeking what is intelligible (80E, 83B) rids itself of violent passions (81A, 83B). Rather than seek bodily pleasure it pursues learning (82C, 83E) and true virtue (82C, 83E), and so joins the company of divinity in the afterlife.

Given Socrates' answer to this question, the whole of the philosopher's life can now be seen as a preparation for death. All of the philosopher's activities aim at achieving the ultimate goal of attaining fellowship with the gods, uninterrupted contemplation and, in short, happiness (81A). The goal is the attainment of happiness; the means is the discipline of *katharsis* (κάθαρσις).[35]

To understand what Socrates means by κάθαρσις or purification we do well to recall what have become his premises. The soul only can attain knowledge. Senses of the body tend to deceive in their representations of the world. Hence, the greater independence of the soul and its thought from the association with the body, the more possible it is for the philosopher to attain the immediate object of its desire, which is the truth. Through understanding the relation between the locus of thought and its object a method for acquiring knowledge and wisdom becomes recognizable.

The means by which that goal is achieved is through moral purification. Purification includes the total collection of practices and habits by which the philosopher frees the soul from the association with the body and its desires

(65A). In this most intimate of settings, Socrates invites his friends to contemplate an image. He likens κάθαρσις to travelling a path (ἀτραπός) which guides the philosopher out of the confusion that accompanies the close association of the body and soul (66B). Note again that Socrates' use of an image at this point in the dialogue is for an *educational purpose*. He communicates to his comrades in a way that will appeal as well to their reason as to their imagination.

Socrates' image of κάθαρσις as a *path* has two parts. The first half of the image represents the singularity of the philosopher's goal. We might speak of this in other terms by saying that the philosopher's will needs to be unified through the ordering of desires. The less valuable desires of the body need to be evaluated as such in comparison to the more valuable desires of the soul. This re-evaluation happens, initially, through the limiting of bodily desires for material objects; food, sex, and clothing are to be despised except in so far as they are necessary (64E). It is the re-evaluation of the relative importance of bodily desires, and the practical consequences of this re-ordering, that Socrates refers to when he talks of disassociating the soul from the body. Following from this, limiting the bodily desires to those which are necessary has the effect of producing a calm within the soul. Apart from achieving this calm, the soul of the philosopher is continually distracted, and its attention divided by various and conflicting unnecessary pleasures and pains that it experiences through the body (84A). Hence, the first part of κάθαρσις is the re-evaluation and limiting of material desire.

The next half of the image of a path represents the skills that are necessary for travelling along the philosophical journey. In this way κάθαρσις also includes the acquisition of *arete*. The initial weakening of physical desire is actually only a means to strengthening the soul's natural capabilities for action. But not all virtues are genuine. The *arete* attained by the many is gained for the sake of other material pleasures:

> My good Simmias, I fear this is not the right exchange to attain virtue, to exchange pleasures for pleasures, pains for pains, fears for fears, the greater for the less coins, but that the only valid currency for which all these things should be exchanged is wisdom. With this we have real courage and moderation and justice and, in a word, true virtue, with wisdom, whether pleasures and fears and all such things be present or absent ... moderation and courage and justice are a purging away of all such things, and wisdom itself is a kind of cleansing or purification. 69A-C

Philosophy is the preparation for death because the goal sought while living can be achieved fully only in dying. As dying is the separation of the soul from the body, for this reason Socrates faces death cheerfully (68B), exhorting his friends to do likewise. And with this, Socrates has answered the riddle which opened the dialogue. Socrates can face death with cheer because he has good reason to believe the bodiless state will mark the beginning of true happiness.

From Socrates' description of philosophy as the practice of death what can we learn about the soul? Foremost, we gain a better understanding of the relationship between the soul and the body. Socrates re-emphasises the fact that the soul can not only be distinguished, but even partially separated from the body in this life. The philosopher is able to loosen the soul's attachment to the body. Secondly, the *value* of the soul is underscored. In the *Phaedo*, much more than in the *Apology*, we find that the good life consists in the struggle to fight against the desires of the body and free the soul to pursue learning. The philosophical life is more like a religious life wherein the soul is engaged in a struggle for deliverance.[21] The philosophical life is a profoundly moral life that requires the total reorientation of the person; the soul must turn from material to immaterial goods; apart from such a turn happiness remains hidden.

CONCLUSION: THE *TOTAL* CONCEPT OF THE ψυχή IN THE *PHAEDO*

Having examined Socrates' four arguments for immortality, his view of the soul of the philosopher in the after-life, and how the philosopher ought to live on earth, we are now in a position to bring together our findings on the character Socrates' view of the soul in the *Phaedo*.

In this chapter we looked at the concept of the soul in the *Phaedo* from a second point of view, and attempted to distinguish features in addition to the *basic* concept. We are now able to add a number of features to the *basic* concept. The soul is, additionally, (i) in its nature non-changing and simple, (ii) invisible and intelligible; (iii) it is divine-like (ruling over the body); (iv) it carries out the activity of imparting life, (v) it performs the operation of recollecting; (vi) the body and soul are separable. From these features Socrates thinks that we can know three others: that the soul is immortal—that is, (vii) that it must pre-exist the body, (viii) survive death, (ix) and never cease to exist.

Alongside Socrates' developing idea of the soul was presented a notion of the transcendent Forms. I make no claim as to whether one came before the other in the sequence of the development of Plato's thought but, in the *Phaedo* at least, the argument for the immortality of the soul relies upon the existence of the Forms. Because of the indivisible and invisible nature of the soul, and because the Forms also have an indivisible nature, by analogy, Socrates argued that the soul is likely to be immortal as the Forms are immortal. The activities of the soul as animating the body or giving life were also made known there. In fact, all of the arguments for immortality in the *Phaedo*, in some way, are based on either of these two ideas: either that the soul is similar to the Forms (arguments 2 and 3), or that the soul gives life (arguments 1 and 4).

The soul is valuable because it is by caring for it and purifying it that we are able to attain happiness. The soul is the most important part of a human being, and the real person. Apart from its health, that is to say, apart from its attaining philosophical virtue, there can be no happiness to speak of. In the *Phaedo* the soul and the body are presented as distinguishable and separable entities. Indeed, given Socrates' determination of a human as a composite of body and soul, it is difficult to see how one could conceive of personal immortality where the body had any lasting involvement at all.

Finally, let us summarize the concept of the soul in the *Phaedo* in terms of the four-fold structure of the concept of the soul highlighted within the introductory chapter. The *nature* of the soul is non-changing and simple, invisible and intelligible, immortal (i.e. pre-existing, surviving death, and never ceasing to exist); it is the self-conscious agent. The soul carries out various *activities* which moderns associate with consciousness including the activities of perceiving, evaluating[22], and recollecting (particularly the Forms which are immaterial objects of cognition); the soul also performs the operation of giving life to the body. In *relation to the body* the soul is that which animates and rules over the body and perceives the material world through the physical senses of the body. The soul acquires moral *arete modifying* the effectiveness of how it performs the various activities natural to the soul; being separable from the body, the soul once purified by philosophy will outlive the body in a state of everlasting happiness.

NOTES

1. That this is the kind of soul Socrates has in mind is emphasised again at the close of the dialogue. In the final death scene Socrates tells his friends not to worry excessively about how the body is to be treated after he has gone: "I have been saying for some time and at some length that after I have drunk the poison I shall no longer be with you but will leave you to go and enjoy some good fortunes of the blessed, but it seems that I have said all this to him in vain in an attempt to reassure you and myself too" (115D).

2. At 70C Plato has "πάλιν γίγνεσθαι" and here Burnet notes how the regular name for this ancient doctrine in later writers is 'παλιγγενεσία'. In early Christian writers such as Hipploytus and Clement this ancient teaching was referred to by the term 'μετενσωμάτωσις' from which, through Latin, we get our English term "reincarnation". Cf. *JB* note 70C8.

3. Jacob Klein points out how Socrates emphasizes this point by saying that there is both an *equal* and *same necessity* (ἴση ἀνάγκη- 76 e 5; ἡ αὐτὴ ἀνάγκη- e 8-9)

for the soul to exist before birth as the Forms. "Still, the necessity of asserting the soul's pre-existence is understood to depend on the presupposed being of the intelligible objects. If they had no being, Socrates says, there would be no point in arguing the pre-existence of our souls (76 e 4;cf. e 7)" (p.130), in his *A Commentary on Plato's* Meno, (Chapel Hill, NC: The University of North Carolina Press, 1965).

4. At 75D.2 the revised Oxford text of the *Phaedo* in *Platonis Opera: Tomus I*, ed. E.A. Duke et. al., (Oxonii: E Typographeo Clarendoniano, 1995), has " ὅ ἔστι" where Burnet's text (1911) has "αὐτο ὅ ἔστιν" . This emendation does not change either the interpretation or the translation of the text.

5. Why this *must* be so is not given a thorough explanation at this point of the dialogue. Socrates brings up the possibility of the soul's gaining knowledge of the forms at the moment of birth (which would then alleviate the necessity of the soul having to exist prior to natural conception). However, he dismisses this suggestion as nonsensical (76D). Incidentally, although St. Augustine (354-430 A.D.) was aware of the Platonic argument on this point, he refused to make a judgment on the question of whether the soul existed before physical conception. Cf. *Confessions*, Bks. I.(7) and IX. (37).

6. We should note Socrates acknowledges that his understanding of the Forms has a significant bearing on the credibility of his belief in an immortal soul. Apart from the veracity of the first theory, the second is not tenable (76E).

7. It appears by this brief dramatic interlude that Plato is emphasizing the role of desire in the pursuit of truth. Rational argument is not enough to persuade Simmias and Cebes; they also require convincing on other levels as well. This theme is returned to at 107A where Simmias again admits that he still has misgivings about the conclusion of the argument, even though he has no reason to disbelieve the arguments themselves. Socrates will eventually turn to a presentation of the immortal soul that appeals more directly to the desire and imagination of his listeners (107Dff).

8. From what Socrates has said so far we would expect him to go on to say that it is by some capability of the soul that these invisible things are grasped. But at this place he introduces a new term. Socrates says that that which always remains the same "can only be grasped by the reasoning of the *mind* (τῷ τῆς διανοίας λογισμῷ)" (79A) (my emphasis). On this text Burnet thinks that there is no distinction being drawn by Socrates' use of 'διάνοια' in preference to 'νοῦς' (mind). He says: "The phrase (τῷ τῆς διανοίας λογισμῷ) means thinking generally as opposed to sense-perception." Cf. *JB* note 79CA3. This change of terminology certainly raises the question as to how Socrates understands the relation between the mind and the soul. Are they the same identical thing? Or is it the case that 'διάνοια' signifies only those features of 'ψυχή' that are specifically associated with *rationality*? I do not think we have enough to go on at this point to determine whether 'mind' and 'soul' are being used interchangeably or not. This passage does, at the least, alert us to the close proximity of meaning that Socrates attaches to these two terms.

9. Socrates is not altogether consistent in his terminology on this point throughout the *Phaedo*. For instance, Socrates sometimes speaks as though the person consists of only two parts, body and soul. (79B, 81A, 106E). In other places Socrates speaks as though there were a third part that went into making up a human being in addition to the body and the soul. In these texts he makes reference to a third part that acts as a kind of

super-ego directing the activities even of the soul (64C, 66B, 88B, 88D). As I shall mention again below, Socrates sometimes speaks of the soul as immaterial and distinct from the body (64C, 92D), while at other times he speaks as though it may be contaminated by corporeality and even become partly visible (81C, 83D).

10. Socrates says that something having the feature of being unchanging also has the feature of immortality in the following way at 79D: "But when the soul investigates by itself and passes into the realm of what is pure, ever existing, immortal and unchanging, and being akin to this, it always stays with it . . ."

11. This argument actually has two parts. The first intends to prove the soul immortal in the sense of unceasing life, the second that the soul is indestructible and that this unceasing life will continue on *indefinitely*. I will look at them both following the order they are presented in the text. I have two reasons for grouping them under one heading; first, because the argument that the soul is indestructible is short and can be examined briefly; second, because this latter argument is logically entailed by the first.

12. In David Gallop's translation of the *Phaedo* (Oxford: Clarendon Press, 1975) he translates 'νοῦς' as 'Intelligence' instead of 'Mind' for the following reason: "The translation 'Intelligence' has been used here as best suited to the idea that things are arranged for the best, which Socrates thought implicit in Anaxagoras' theory . . . but which 'mind' and 'intellect' fail, in different ways, to convey. 'Intelligence' (*nous*) should be understood here as a substance term. It is the faculty of thought, or that which thinks, rather than a mental quality, such as 'sagacity' or 'good sense'" (p.174).

13. Socrates expresses incredulity at those who suppose a materialist view of causality is sufficient. He says that while material causes do explain some things they cannot account for *why* it is that things happen the way they do. Socrates takes this as obvious, for example, as when considering the cause of human action. Reflecting on his own actions of the past weeks he scoffs at the possibility that a material explanation could account for why he allowed himself to be tried and, ultimately, executed by the Athenians: "For by the dog, I think these sinews and bones could long ago have been in Megara or among the Boeotians, taken there by my belief as to the best course, if I had not thought it more right and honorable to endure whatever penalty the city ordered rather than escape and run away" (98E-99A).

14. Socrates does not give a detailed explanation of the way that he thinks the Forms act as causes, and he warned earlier that he would not provide such detail when he told Cebes "I will not insist on the precise nature of the relationship [between the Forms and their effects]" (100D). For a discussion of what might be conjectured regarding Socrates' presentation of the relation between the Forms and particulars at this point in the dialogue see Gallop, *ibid*., 182-184.

15. I have benefited from David Bostock's comments on these texts which are given in his study, *ibid*.,187-189.

16. Cf. *LSJ* s.v. ἀπόλλυμι I.1.

17. Cf. *LSJ* s.v. ἀνώλεθρος I.2.

18. I say 'presumably' because the implications of Socrates' comments at 81A quoted above seem to lead to this conclusion. If the soul of the philosopher makes its way to what is invisible and like itself, and if there are also souls of other philosophers

that have undergone a similar purification, then it would seem to follow that these like-purified souls would find themselves in a common fellowship.

19. I should like to point out that, through the telling of the Myth of the afterlife, Socrates is doing much more than attempting to outline a logical sequence of ideas. He is endeavouring to persuade his friends to live a good life. The Myth is part of a larger *moral* exhortation wherein Socrates prevails upon his friends to watch over themselves, and that means to take care of their souls. Socrates reasons that because we have good evidence for the immortal soul, certain moral virtues should be sought, which in turn bring with them good dispositions:

> . . . a man should be of good cheer (θαρρεῖν) about his own soul, if during life he has ignored the pleasures of the body and its ornamentation as of no concern to him and doing him more harm than good, but has seriously concerned himself with the pleasures of learning, and adorned his soul not with alien but with its own ornaments, namely, moderation, righteousness, courage, freedom and truth, and in that state awaits his journey to the underworld. 114D-115A.

Socrates has concluded his Myth by admonishing his friends to turn from bodily pleasures to the pleasures of the soul. Having sought to attain virtue in this life the philosopher can expect to face death with confidence. These ethical exhortations recall the spirit of Socrates' remarks made before the Athenian jury at the end of the *Apology*.

20. According to Burnet, Socrates' notion of *katharsis* seems to be ultimately derived from the Pythagorian doctrine (cf. *JB* note 61A3). Gallop says of the general significance of *katharsis* within the dialogue that, "The concept of purification pervades the whole dialogue, and strengthens the Pythagorean associations suggested by its characterization and setting. . . It is ironical that Athen's concern for her 'purity' should have delayed Socrates' death. His execution was to afford the release of soul from body in which his own 'purification' would be perfected" *ibid.*, 75. Jacob Klein identifies rebirth, purification, as well as related to musical topics, as the main Pythagorean themes that appear within the dialogue. In his footnote (nos.52) he also provides references to ancient and modern commentary on these themes within the *Phaedo, ibid.*, 125-127.

21. On this point Robinson notes the significant difference between Socrates' conception of purification and the view dominant within the popular Greek mystery religions of his time: "But if [Socrates] has incorporated the religious notion of purification into his thinking, it is no ritual cleansing, no superstitious placation of the powers that be with meticulous ceremony. True purification is the life of philosophy . . . or love of learning, or 'philosophic virtue'; all amount to the same thing. Whatever esoteric creeds may have taught, the notion is transformed into something new by Socratic intellectualism. There is no true virtue without intelligence . . ." *TMR*, 24.

22. It is interesting to notice what does not emerge from this study; namely, an elaborated account of the *will*. For that one must wait, most fully, for St. Augustine.

Chapter Four

Alternative Treatments of the ψυχή in Four of Plato's 'Middle' Dialogues

INTRODUCTION

In this chapter I consider a number of alternative treatments of the soul. In the course of Plato's dialogues we find a variety of conceptions of the soul presented by the character Socrates, from the immortal and tripartite soul of the *Republic* to the apparently mortal and eros-led soul of the *Symposium*. In what follows I examine Plato's representation of Socrates' view of the soul through four of Plato's dialogues; this is a useful exercise because it provides us with the opportunity to draw comparisons and contrasts between Plato's works. I turn to what are often called the middle dialogues in what is sometimes regarded as the chronological sequence in which they were written[1] (*Meno, Symposium*, [*Phaedo*], *Republic, Phaedrus*)[2] with the intent of clarifying what has already been discovered about the soul of the *Phaedo*.

MENO: RECOLLECTION AS THE BASIS FOR SHOWING THE IMMORTAL ψυχή

Although the doctrine of the immortal soul does not figure prominently in the overall discussion of the *Meno*, it does appear at a rather significant juncture. As we may recall, Meno is an accomplished orator and asks Socrates early on in the dialogue whether he thinks virtue (ἀρετή) is something that can be taught (70A). Socrates does not know the answer to this, but is capable of helping Meno to realize his question depends upon another. Discovering whether virtue is teachable assumes a knowledge of what virtue is in itself (71B). From then on the main problem that animates the dialogue is Meno and Socrates' search for a common definition of excellence or virtue (ἀρετή). After a series of failed attempts at saying what virtue is, Meno finally admits that he has come to his wits' end, and finds himself stunned in a state of perplexity (ἀπορία) (80A). Because of Socrates' questions he is unable to say even what virtue is—Meno states his new dilemma by posing a question: How is it possible to find what you are searching for unless you already know beforehand what it is you are looking for so as to identify it when it is found? (80D) This is Meno's paradox.

To escape the logical puzzle Socrates proposes a teaching which includes the theory of the immortal soul. He recounts for his friend the teaching of priests, priestesses, and divinely inspired poets who say that the soul is not only immortal, but also that it has been born many times. This means that the soul existed before it came into a body, allowing for time beforehand for the soul to gain knowledge of many subjects (e.g. geometry, in the case of the slave boy). Thus, the doctrine of reincarnation is suggested as a means of overcoming the impasse that Meno and Socrates have found themselves in. Socrates offers the soul's immortality as a way of explaining how learning is actually a process of recollecting things already known before birth. If what is commonly called learning is better deemed recollection (ἀνάμνησις), then Meno's paradox is dissolved; the soul need not search for what it does not in any way know, since it merely has to recognize and call to mind knowledge that was *previously* acquired.

In the *Meno* the doctrine of the immortal soul has both ethical and epistemological implications. On the first count, actions in this life have enduring moral repercussions. Because the soul lives on past death, Socrates admonishes Meno that a person must live as piously as possible in this life (81B). If one fails to live well now punishments await in the future. Secondly, the doctrine of an immortal soul helps to justify his account of learning as remembering. Since the soul existed in a pre-bodily state Socrates can resolve the contradiction pointed to in Meno's paradox by saying that, as a matter of fact, "there is nothing that is not learned" (81C).

SYMPOSIUM: VICARIOUS IMMORTALITY AND THE SEARCH FOR THE BEAUTIFUL

The *Symposium* is a series of encomia delivered in praise of the god Love. In this dialogue Socrates and six of his friends gather to celebrate Agathon's victory at the dramatic contest held during the Lemon Festival at Athens. Instead of spending yet another evening in heavy drinking, at Phaedrus' prompting they give the night over to conversation. Eryximachus arranges his guests in a speaking order and each in turn delivers a hymn of praise to the god. Socrates agrees to go along with the proposal by wryly saying the only thing that he does understand is "the art of erotics (τὰ ἐρωτικά)" (177D). Each person in the group then takes his turn. Socrates delivers his encomium in the form of a recitation of a speech that he earlier heard from Diotima, a wise woman with magical powers (201D). It is during Socrates' speech that the subject of the nature of the soul and its immortality comes up. He recalls how Diotima defined *eros* as the desire for continual possession of good things (206A), and the desire to reproduce and "give birth in the presence of beauty" (206E). But what can that mean? Socrates clarifies her meaning (a little) by saying that lovers cannot but help desire immortality alongside the good they perceive in the object of their affections. The desire for sexual union, which draws lover and beloved into the act of reproduction, is nothing other than an expression of the desire for immortality (206E). There is a natural love of self-preservation. In short, by means of love the mortal nature of humans and animals alike seeks so far as is possible "to exist forever and be immortal (ἀει εἶναι καί ἀθάνατος)" (207D).

But what sort of immortality is it that mortals actually can or do attain? Diotima points out that both body and soul are in constant flux: the body, because its physical features are ever coming into and going out of being; the soul, because its habits, desires, and knowledge are always changing (208A). She goes on to add that some people are pregnant with the desire for immortality in their bodies, while others are pregnant in their souls. Immortality is gained by exerting influence to cause change in the world which can be recognized by others. Producing physical offspring no less than deeds of glory are each, in their own way, the means to achieve a lasting memory of oneself (208Dff); through both means people show forth their striving for perpetual existence. Significantly, in the *Symposium* the only kind of immortality open for humans is that gained vicariously.

Socrates then gives a systematic explanation of the desire for immortality and the various ways that love manifests its presence within people. Though all immortality is achieved through the memory of others, there are distinguishable degrees or kinds of longing within people. He reports how Diotima disclosed to himself the ladder of love: an image of the ascent that must be climbed by all who are to rise to the object of greatest longing of all. People pass through longing for individual bodies, bodies in general, souls, and only after these arrive at the peak of the ladder. The greatest longing is revealed as the yearning for the Form of the Beautiful itself; the Form of Beauty is that for the sake of which all other things are ultimately desired (210A-210E).

What is striking in Socrates' account of the soul in the *Symposium*, in relation to the account found in the *Phaedo* and each of the other dialogues we are looking at in this chapter (with the qualified exception of the *Meno*),³ is the presence of a doctrine of the transcendent Forms but without a doctrine of the immortal individual human soul. For the vast majority of people the only completion of their longing for immortality is to be achieved through sexual reproduction. Their memory and something of their physical body lives on through offspring. Far fewer people (of the likes of Alcestis and Achilles) achieve a kind of immortality through the remembrance of their noble deeds (208D). Fewer still, such as the great poets and lawmakers of Greece, gain a measure of immortality through the ideas and arguments that they pass on to those who study their works or live under their legislation (209Cff). To the philosopher alone, it seems, is a continuation of their individual soul even suggested, and that only tentatively (212B). The philosophers are the ones who rise above the love of beautiful bodies, rise above the love of fine souls and laws, to gaze upon the Form of Beauty itself (210Aff). Plato has a highly developed account of the Forms in the *Symposium* to which he appeals in his account of eros within the soul; but he draws no further conclusions about the soul's immortality here.

REPUBLIC: THE ψυχή IS IMMORTAL AND HAS THREE PARTS

In the *Republic* we find Plato's magnificent and most sustained treatment of the nature of justice. The dialogue is a discussion of the nature of justice and the relationship between the philosopher and the political community. In it, Socrates defends the merits of justice: he considers whether justice is in and of itself better than injustice (cf.358D and 612C), and concludes that justice rightly is praised for bestowing good things on those who possess it (612D). In the *Republic*, philosophy vindicates justice and the value of leading a philosophical life by proving that justice and the search for a just regime within the soul and within the life of the community brings with it its own rewards that far outweigh the perceived benefits of injustice.

In order to evaluate the merits of justice, however, Socrates must first help his friends to discover what it is. To discover that they turn to an examination of a city in speech, which, Socrates says, is an image of the human soul writ large (cf. 368E and 435C). In viewing the perfectly good city and the perfectly good man, Socrates says: "perhaps searching them out side by side, and rubbing them as though fire-sticks, we would make justice to burst into flame, and becoming clear, we would confirm it for ourselves" (435A). With a view to understanding the nature of justice, Socrates turns to describe the nature of the soul.

In the *Republic* Socrates provides a detailed account of all four aspects of the soul that, in Chapter One, we said together comprise the concept of a human soul. As for the nature of the soul, in the *Republic* it is tripartite. In Socrates' treatment of the *polis* he found three distinct classes of citizens comprise the population. A single human has the same forms in his soul as can be found in the naturally occurring political organization of the perfect city that was constructed in speech by the character Socrates. After much argumentation, Socrates eventually feels confident to assert that they have together discovered a form and disposition (εἴδη τε καὶ ἤθη) corresponding to each of the three distinct forms found in the city (435E).

First is the calculating part of the soul, the part that is capable of reckoning and reasoning about the best course of action to take. This part of the soul is analogous to the ruling class in the city. Second is the irrational or desiring part of the soul. This is the part of the soul's nature by which it loves, hungers, thirsts and is agitated by the other desires (439D), analogous to the money-makers and merchants within the city who spend their time accumulating wealth. Third is the spirited part of the soul. This is analogous to the warrior class. This spirited part sometimes makes war against the desires and reproaches the man for desiring base things. As an example of the activity of the spirited part Socrates recounts the story of a man who once noticed corpses of executed prisoners lying beside a public executioner. Seeing the bodies this traveler experienced two kinds of desire. One was an impulse to gawk at the dead; the other to turn away—since looking upon dead bodies is a shameful thing to do (339E). What is it that initiates action in the face of divided inclinations? For Socrates it is this spirited part of the soul. It is roused against (or for) the desiring part whenever it is in conflict with the calculating part of the soul (440A). Furthermore, it is this part of the soul's nature that helps a man to endure hardships and suffering for the sake of justice or for achieving ends that the calculating part considers good.

The soul is one with three distinct parts. In Socrates' description of the nature of the soul as tripartite we also gain insight into his view of the soul's activities or operations. Each of the three parts is responsible for carrying out a different activity that is performed by the soul. In the calculating part the soul's reasoning is highlighted. In the second, irrational part of the soul, we can see the activity of desiring most clearly. Lastly, it is in some relation of the activity of the calculating and the spirited parts that we are able to identify the activity of the soul's willing or bringing-into-effect what has been determined as the best course of action by the calculating character of the soul.

Later in the dialogue Socrates treats early education, and here the relation between the soul and the body is given some consideration. The soul and the body are both distinct and separable parts of a human being. Although the body is clearly subordinate in value and influence in regards to the education of the soul (403D), the education of the body is also important. In Socrates' description of the philosopher's education, the body has a determinative role, particularly in the education of the young. The educational goal of early education is to habituate the desire and the will through training by music and poetry (401Aff) and gymnastics (403Dff).

Socrates likewise has a good deal to say about the virtues and vices in the *Republic*. The catalogue of virtues and vices are the possible variations of the habits and states of soul that serve, principally, to modify the soul's activities, but also its relation to the body. Hence, in the *Republic* the soul that has virtue is able to carry out its own operations well, while the soul lacking virtue is not able to do so. Each of the parts have a different and corresponding virtue. The calculating part is virtuous when it acquires *wisdom*, that is, the ability to discern what is good in every situation (442C). The vice of the calculating part is ignorance and stupidity. The desiring part of the soul is virtuous when it has *moderation* or, the ability to desire what the calculating part determines is good to seek after (410E). Lack of virtue of this part of the soul is easily recognizable. When the desiring part leads the direction of the soul, it gives itself over to pleasure and seeking money (442A). As a further consequence a man becomes easily irritable (411B). This is a link to the spirited part of the soul. When it is excellent it has *courage*, and the ability to arouse the soul to persevere through hardships for the sake of what is good (410B; 441D). When filled with vice, the improperly trained spirited aspect will find itself acting harshly (i.e. irritable), and lose any natural concern for learning and philosophy. Lastly, *justice* is the outcome of all the parts of the soul's essence working in harmony (441D).

Socrates' argument for the immortality of the soul in Book 10 deserves some mention. He begins with a definition of good and bad; what brings benefit and saves is good, what destroys and corrupts is bad (608E). Everything, he says, has its own particular corruption and sickness that is suited to its own nature. As rust is to iron, so rot is to wood. In these examples Socrates is pointing out that things can be destroyed only by an evil that is particularly related to itself (609A). Sickness particular to the body is disease. But as he points out, not even bad foods can make the body sick unless the food introduces the sort of disease that is particular to the body (610A). Eventually he draws the general conclusion that *one thing is never destroyed by the evil particular to another* (610A). The application of this principle means that the sickness of the body can have no direct harmful influence upon the soul. Socrates admits that there are things that make the soul bad: injustice, licentiousness, cowardice, and lack of learning, each qualify as vices which damage the soul (608B). Do these vices actually *destroy* the soul? They do not. Socrates observes: when a man is caught doing injustice he is not destroyed, but only harmed, and is able to continue living. Thus, from this empirical observation, and the previous conclusion that each thing has its own evil, Socrates surmises that if vice cannot destroy the soul then nothing will (611A).

PHAEDRUS: THE TRIPARTITE ψυχή IS AN UNMOVED MOVER

Socrates' most important discussion of the soul in the *Phaedrus* is found in the middle of his second 'Great Speech' of that dialogue (243E-257B). Socrates and Phaedrus have left the city walls to find a quiet place together to read. They have ventured into the countryside so that Phaedrus may read aloud to Socrates a newly completed speech by Lysias, the famous Athenian rhetorician and speech-maker, on the topic of love (ἐρωτικός). After listening to the speech Socrates gives a reply (237Cff) and a lengthy speech of his own (237B-241D). Immediately after concluding his first speech, however, Socrates retracts his statements and sets out upon a second attempt. He says that the reason why he must take back his first speech is because he acted foolishly and impiously (242D). He had spoken as though love were something evil; with regret, he now regards this as a terrible thing to have said (242E).

Socrates' second and celebrated speech is a Palinode to Love. In it he recounts his former position that madness is an evil (244A) and goes on to describe the types of madness and their benefits to Greece in both public and private spheres. Socrates then considers: why do the gods allow madness to be given to humans at all? Surprisingly it is so that humans may achieve the greatest good fortune (245B). To understand how madness can bring about the greatest fortune to humans Socrates says we must first comprehend the nature of the soul. It is at this point Socrates turns to his proof of immortality.

His basic argument is as follows. He claims that whatever always has motion is immortal (τὸ γὰρ ἀει κίνητον ἀθάνατον). Now some things move of their own accord, and some things are moved by other things. A first principle (ἀρχή) is that which moves things by its own accord and itself never comes into being. And since first principles never come into being, Socrates further supposes that they must also never perish and go out of being (245D). An unmoved first principle is immortal because the negation of this would lead to an absurd conclusion, namely, if ever a first principle were to die then the whole universe would collapse (245E). The universe would collapse because without the existence of unmoved sources of motion there would be nothing left to impart motion throughout the structure of the physical world. Doubtless this cessation of all motion is unlikely.

But how exactly are we to recognize the effects of an ἀρχή in the material universe? Socrates says that every body that has its source of motion outside itself is devoid of soul, whereas whatever is self-moved is en-souled (ἔμψυχον). In other words, we recognize the effects of the first principles in the universe by observing bodies that have self-generated motion. From his explanation of motion in the world, and the identification of first principles with the cause of motion, Socrates is able to succinctly summarize his understanding of the nature or essence of soul. In short, since whatever is self-moving is immortal "this very thing [i.e. self-motion] is [or, *is of*] the essence and definition of soul (ψυχῆς οὐσίαν τε καὶ λόγον τοῦτον αὐτόν)" (245E). Thus, the soul is something which is both self-moving and immortal (246A).

Having spoken of its immortality, Socrates fills in the concept of the soul by means of an image. It is much like a charioteer with two horses. The charioteer attempts to guide his horses, but finds one of them difficult to master and make obedient to his commands. The charioteer represents the reasoning part of the soul. One of the horses is the noble desire within the soul, the other, the irascible and rebellious appetite. The role of the charioteer, of course, is to rule over his horses and lead them in the best direction. While doing this, however, he is constantly quarrelling with the unruly horse which symbolizes the base appetites that try to re-route the direction of the whole chariot and the whole soul.

The soul in the *Phaedrus* is immortal because it is self-moving. And we have seen how Socrates believes that that which has soul within it is imparted motion. Like the *Republic* the soul has three parts. Socrates does not in the *Phaedrus* address the question (as we shall see) that he does in the *Republic*; namely, whether all three parts of the soul are immortal. Also, there is a different emphasis on the nature of the soul than that given in the *Republic*. In the *Phaedrus* the main conflict experienced within a person is between the base appetite and the reasoning part of the soul, and the noble appetite has a rather underdeveloped role to play in Socrates' chief image of the soul. Whereas in the *Republic*, the role of the spirited part of the soul's nature was thoroughly described, as was the catalogue of virtues and vices that corresponded to each of the various parts that together make up the soul's essence.

CONCLUSION: ALTERNATIVE TREATMENTS OF THE ψυχή CONTRASTED WITH THE *PHAEDO*

Compared to the treatment of the soul in the *Phaedo*, Socrates' treatment of the soul in the *Meno* is minimal. The soul in the *Meno* is associated with the moral character or habits of a person; in this sense the nature or essence of the soul as the centre of rational awareness is reaffirmed here (as it is in the *Apology*). However, the soul is also associated more directly with the activity of recollection. It is from the activity of recollecting that Socrates believes he is able to show that the soul must have a pre-bodily existence and be immortal. It is a soul that experiences birth and death in an unending cycle of reincarnation.

There is also a significant difference in the way the soul is treated in the *Meno* as compared to the *Phaedo*. For instance, Socrates makes use of the arguments for immortality in at least three ways differently in the *Meno* than in the *Phaedo*. First, in the *Meno* argument for immortality there is no recourse to the doctrine of the immaterial Forms. We recall that in Socrates' view the doctrine of the Forms played a very significant role in the argumentation for immortality in the *Phaedo*. Second, in the *Meno* Socrates presents 'learning as recollecting' as an argument that independently establishes immortality. From this activity of the soul alone Socrates thinks that it must both have preexisted and be immortal. In the *Phaedo* Socrates seems to have revised his views on the value of this argument. At the writing of the *Phaedo* the soul's operation of learning is directly the basis only for the soul's pre-existence, but *not* its post-existence. The third difference is that in the *Phaedo* Socrates considers an objection to his argument from the activity of learning that he seems not to have yet anticipated in the *Meno*. Recall in the *Phaedo's* version of the argument how Cebes asks Socrates if knowledge could have been acquired at the very moment of birth — and so account for their observations on learning without positing pre-existence. In the *Phaedo* this objection is addressed, while in the *Meno* the possibility is not even raised (compare *Men.* 86A with *Phdo.* 76C). In short, in the *Phaedo* there are both new improvements to the argument that the soul's activity of learning shows forth its immortality, as well as new objections considered that do not appear within the *Meno*. In my opinion, such differences in the treatment of the soul and the arguments for personal immortality are likely evidence suggesting a development in Plato's thinking about the problem, on which grounds we can have some confidence of the notion that the *Meno* was written before the *Phaedo*. However, such conjectures should be taken as only that.

Next, what sort of soul is presented in the *Symposium*? Here we find a very incomplete presentation of the soul. In the dialogue the soul of the philosopher is able to perform the operation of reasoning about the Forms, but Socrates makes no argument for the affinity between the soul and the indivisible Forms as he does in the third argument in the *Phaedo* that we looked at in Chapter Three. Also interesting to note is the relation of the soul to the body in the *Symposium*. In the *Phaedo* the life of the philosopher was depicted in terms of a conflict between the desires of the body (which seek after material goods) and the desires of the soul (which seek after immaterial goods): thus the conflict for the philosopher is between body and soul. In the *Symposium* this is not the case. The desires of body and soul are placed upon a continuum from good to best. In the *Symposium* it seems most unlikely that the philosopher could ever rise to the love of the sublime intellectual objects without first having some *eros* for the lower.

There is a new common denominator between the two kinds of desire, a new mediating attraction which links the lower and the higher in man. The presence of *eros* is now recognized within both kinds of longing. The task for the philosopher in the *Symposium* is not to reject the desires of the body, which seemed the case in the *Phaedo*, but to use them as a means of ascending to objects more fitting for the soul. Regarding the acquired states and habits that qualify the activities of the soul and its relation to the body, again there is very little said about these in this dialogue. We might remark that the chief virtue of the philosopher in this dialogue is a strong *eros*. But it is unclear whether the degree of longing felt within a person is something that may be cultivated or something given to them by nature. What is distinctive about the soul in the *Symposium* is that its capability for intellectual contemplation is dependent upon its degree of *eros*. Also, a person may impress their identity upon the memory of others, but it does not appear, at least not for the vast multitudes of human beings, that their soul could possibly live forever.

Turning to the *Republic*, we have found that there exist similarities in the conception of the soul in this dialogue to the *total* concept of the soul in the *Phaedo*. Most prominently, of course, is the fact that the soul in both dialogues is an immortal soul. Moreover, the value of the soul and of its education is also emphasized in both dialogues, as well as the view that the soul's immortality has ethical implications for how a philosopher ought to live in this life.

But there are also a great many dissimilarities. To begin with, Socrates' conception of the soul in the *Republic* differs from the *Phaedo* in that the nature of the soul in the *Republic* is tripartite instead of simple. In Book 4 Socrates leads Glaucon step by step in a reasoned argument to identify each of the distinct parts; the calculating or reasoning, the desiring, and the spirited parts together make up the essence of the soul. Although Socrates spends a good deal of time describing the three-part soul, and indeed relies upon it to make coherent the analogous description of the three parts of the *polis*, at one point he acknowledges the possibility that this account too may be inaccurate. In Book 10, when Socrates offers his proof for the soul's immortality, he raises the following objection: he admits that it is not easy "for a thing to be eternal that is both composed out of many things and whose composition is not of the finest, as the soul now looked to us" (611B). Socrates then qualifies all his previous descriptions of the three-part soul by saying that they have been looking at the soul as it appears to them now, not as it really is. As we see the soul now, he confesses, we see it in a condition of countless evils. To properly understand it one must look elsewhere. One must look towards "its love of wisdom, and recognize what it lays hold of and with what sort of things it longs to keep company on the grounds that it is akin to the divine and immortal and what *is* always. . ." (611E). This late qualification, in the end, seems to bring Socrates' account of the nature of the soul much closer to that given in the *Phaedo* than we had earlier supposed. It brings the account of the soul closer to that given in the *Phaedo* because Socrates has suggested that only one part of the soul is immortal, the reasoning part.

Moreover, in the *Republic* Socrates' account of the relation of the soul to the body is further developed than that given in the *Phaedo*. In the *Republic* the soul is distinct from the body but, unlike the *Phaedo*, the *Republic* clearly represents the conflict within a human being as occurring between the various *parts* of the soul. The struggle to become good and wise is a struggle within the soul to bring together into a working harmony the calculating and the desiring parts, and to have the spirited part continually strengthening and encouraging this union between reason and desire. The various states of soul that modify the activities of the soul are also much more fully elaborated in the *Republic*. Each part of the soul has a corresponding virtue: wisdom, courage, moderation, and the whole soul is said to have justice when each of the parts work together in their proper function. Such a detailed catalogue of virtues and vices is absent from within the *Phaedo*.

There are three interesting points to note when comparing the conception of the soul in the *Phaedrus* to that given in the *Phaedo*. First, like the *Phaedo* the soul is sometimes referred to as "mind" in the *Phaedrus*, as in when Socrates refers to "the mind of the philosopher" (ἡ τοῦ φιλοσόφου διάνοια) during his second speech (*Phdr*. 249C). Socrates' references to 'διάνοια' as a term for the individual soul are always in places when the activity or operation of rationality and the rational part of the soul's nature is being highlighted, except once. In the *Phaedrus* Socrates refers to the soul by means of the term 'διάνοια' when specifically pointing to the irrational activity and *irrational* part of the soul (265E). Hence, in the *Phaedrus* Socrates either makes a slip or changes his terminology as, perhaps, a means of underscoring the fact that the soul has both a rational and an irrational part to its nature. Second, also in regards to the nature of the soul in the *Phaedrus*, Socrates posits a conception of the soul's nature in this dialogue in a unique way. He says that whatever is self-moving is immortal, and that "this very thing is the essence and definition of soul (ψυχῆς οὐσίαν τε καὶ λόγον τοῦτον αὐτόν)" (245E). In this dialogue alone of those we have studied is self-motion specifically singled out as the nature or essence of the soul, and that by which we can give an account of what it is. Lastly, in the *Phaedrus* Socrates makes use of the theory of recollection to draw attention to the soul's activity of learning, but puts far less emphasis on the argument here than in either the *Phaedo* or the *Meno*.

NOTES

1. The relative chronology of the dialogues which I have listed is based upon the evaluation of stylometric and other evidence by David Ross in *Plato's Theory of Ideas, ibid.*, 10. Ross claims to provide only a probable order of the texts, and whether or not this is the actual chronological order of the dialogues is not in the first instance relevant to my own argument. For my purposes I have chosen to look at these particular dialogues because of their *thematic*, and not chronological, similarities to the *Phaedo*. For a good review of the methods and findings of 19th and 20th century research in stylometry and its bearing on the chronology of Plato's dialogues see Leonard Brandwood's essay "Stylometry and Chronology" in *The Cambridge Companion to Plato*, ed. Richard Kraut, (Cambridge: CUP, 1992), 90–120.

2. All translations in this chapter are my own. The editions I am using are as follows: R.W. Sharples' modified version of Bluck's Cambridge edition printed alongside Sharples' translation and commentary on the *Meno*, (Warminister, Wiltshire, UK: Aris and Phillips, Ltd., 1985); Kenneth Dover's edition of the *Symposium*, (Cambridge: CUP, 2002); I have referred to the text of the *Republic* printed alongside Paul Shorey's translation (in two volumes) in the Loeb edition (Cambridge, Massachusetts: Harvard University Press, 1937); lastly, I make reference to the modified version of Burnet's Oxford text printed alongside C.J. Rowe's translation and commentary of the *Phaedrus*, (Warminister, Wiltshire, UK: Aris and Phillips, Ltd., 1986).

3. See R. W. Sharples' comments in his introduction to his translation of the *Meno* where he lists the various ways that the presentation of the forms given in the *Meno* differs from that given in the *Phaedo*, *Symposium* and *Republic*, *ibid.*, 11–14.

Chapter Five

General Conclusion

SUMMARY OF THE FINDINGS OF THIS STUDY

We are ready to revisit the primary and secondary questions of this study, some of my own methodological procedures that I have employed, and the conclusions that I have come to.

In Chapter One I stated that the primary question I sought to answer was methodological. I asked: by what method might we best interpret Socrates' comments about the soul in the *Phaedo*? I answered that the best way to do this was to separate Socrates' comments into basic and total concepts. The subsequent chapters have been, for the most part, an attempt to substantiate this claim by illustrating its efficacy or explanatory power. I have tried to show that this interpretive tool can help us to answer other secondary questions that fall into two groups. First, by analyzing Socrates' comments about the soul in the *Phaedo* from the point of view of the *basic* and *total* concepts I have been able to identify something about the nature of the arguments in the *Phaedo*, their relation to each other, and something of their relation to arguments about the soul in a series of other Platonic dialogues. Second, I have been able to identify the features of the soul presented throughout the *Phaedo* which I will list below. In addition to this, I asserted that any conception of the human soul must include four elements: an account of the soul's nature, activities, relation to the body, and the acquired states and habits that modify any of the other aspects.

In Chapters Two and Three I analyzed the concept of the soul in the *Phaedo* from two different points of view; first, by noting those features given by Socrates that were not used by him to show forth either its pre-existence or post-existence, and second, by studying those that included more than the basic concept. After applying this interpretive method, at the end of Chapter Two I concluded that the *basic* concept of the soul in the *Phaedo* was as follows: the defining characteristic or what makes up the essence of the soul is that it is the conscious person; it performs the activities of thinking, and desiring after the knowledge of immaterial objects of cognition; it is the locus of moral habits and dispositions; the soul is distinct from the body, and (while joined to the body) attains excellence by striving to avoid preoccupation with the desires of the body, or with objects of bodily cognition, as much is humanly possible.

In Chapter Three I articulated features of the soul in addition to the *basic* concept. I summarized the concept of the soul in the *Phaedo* in terms of the four-fold structure of the concept of the soul I highlighted: the *nature* of the soul is non-changing and simple, invisible and intelligible, immortal (i.e. pre-existing, surviving death, and never ceasing to exist); it is the self-conscious agent. The soul carries out various *activities* which moderns associate with consciousness including the activities of perceiving, evaluating, and recollecting (particularly the Forms which are immaterial objects of cognition); the soul also performs the operation of giving life to the body. In *relation to the body* the soul is that which animates and rules over the body and perceives the material world through the physical senses of the body. The soul acquires moral *arete modifying* the effectiveness of how it performs the various activities natural to the soul; being separable from the body, the soul once purified by philosophy will outlive the body in a state of everlasting happiness. This is the complete concept of the soul in the *Phaedo*, and represents the primary finding of our study.

In Chapter Four I briefly looked at the arguments for immortality given within four other Platonic dialogues. Reviewing Plato's conceptions of the soul in the *Meno, Symposium, Republic* and *Phaedrus* I tried to make explicit the alternative conceptions of the soul within these dialogues. By this exercise I was able to highlight places of similarities and dissimilarities between Plato's concepts and arguments in the *Phaedo* and those within these four other dialogues which are generally considered to have been written during the second or middle period of Plato's writing.

How has our exegesis helped us to interpret Plato? Let us clarify the two main secondary findings that I believe have followed from our procedure with regards to the interpretation of Plato's thought about the soul.

The first secondary finding is concerning the *kinds of arguments* employed in the *Phaedo*, and may be stated briefly. Through this analysis of the *Phaedo* I have been able to illustrate that Socrates is making arguments about *features of the soul*, and not aiming to prove the existence of the individual human soul *per se*. We have seen that Socrates attempts to prove the soul is immortal by showing that the soul has certain features: it is these features themselves which provide basis for belief in the soul's immortality.

The second secondary finding is more complex. In terms of the relation between the arguments for immortality, I have been able to show that *there is a development of the complexity in the arguments themselves*. If Plato did not change his views on the conception of the soul throughout the course of writing the dialogue, he certainly presents it as though the character Socrates' views had done as much. We saw (in Chapter Three) the way that the character Socrates seems to be improving upon his arguments by making additions (e.g. the first to the second argument) and wholesale revisions (e.g. the fourth argument as compared to the first).[1] Whether or not Plato wrote this way in the *Phaedo* because of pedagogical aims or because he had not fully thought through the entirety of the argument beforehand is a question I do not need to decide upon. What seems clear enough is that there is a change and a refinement in Socrates' initial ability to describe the aspects of the soul such that his arguments become more sophisticated as the conversation of the dialogue carries on.[2]

Moreover, when we compare the conceptions of the soul in the *Phaedo* to Plato's other dialogues, my findings seem consistent with or as confirming the generally accepted chronological order of the composition of the dialogues.[3] I think there are reasonably good grounds to believe that there is development within Plato's view of the soul throughout the so-called middle dialogues, although I make no claim to have demonstrated such a view myself. What is important to note here is that Plato's *Phaedo* represents a highpoint in his developing conception of the soul, though it is by no means the summit. There are many questions and ambiguities that Plato simply does not address in the *Phaedo* that are resolved elsewhere – as, most notably, in the *Republic*. For example, in the *Phaedo* Plato provides a very rudimentary treatment of the virtues and vices of the soul; in the *Republic* this fourth aspect of his concept is refined and given a systematic treatment. Also, in both the *Republic* and *Phaedrus* Plato feels confident to describe the soul's nature in terms of three parts. By reference to the soul's three-part nature Plato is able to give a much more elaborate expression of the soul's activities (reasoning, willing, desiring) and acquired states (virtues and vices).

I say that Plato *appears* confident to discuss the three-part soul in these two dialogues. There are difficulties inherent in this view that he is aware of. As Socrates himself admits (*Rep*.611B), a three-part soul makes immortality something more difficult to prove. In the *Phaedo* the arguments for immortality are prominent, and one gets the sense that they are being worked out for the first time. By the time of the *Republic* the situation is quite different. Plato's clarity about the soul has been sharpened and there is familiarity, as he has Socrates mention, with those "other arguments" for immortality—presumably referring to those already given in the *Phaedo* (cf. *Rep.* 611B). In the *Republic* and *Phaedrus* Plato does not need to insist that an invisible soul must be indivisible or simple; he has found new arguments that do not depend on the kind of distinctions between body and soul argued for in the *Phaedo*. My own findings appear to be consistent with the view that the *Phaedo* was written before both the *Phaedrus* and the *Republic*.

Although the *Phaedo* looks to be written earlier than these two dialogues, it displays a considerable maturity on the subject of the soul and a development when compared to the so-called "Socratic dialogues", and even when compared with the *Meno*. The Socrates of the *Apology* does not know whether the soul is immortal, and he is not even willing to say that he believes it will survive bodily death. The Socrates of the *Phaedo* has gone far beyond the Socrates of the *Apology* in his willingness to affirm and offer arguments for belief in the immortal soul. One of the arguments for immortality in the *Phaedo* has direct resemblance to that given in the *Meno*, although the former is much more thorough. In the *Phaedo* Socrates answers objections to the argument that did not even arise in the *Meno* and gives a completely new version of the argument from the activity of learning which incorporates a doctrine of the Forms.

THE MORAL VALUE OF SOCRATES' ARGUMENTS FOR IMMORTALITY IN THE *PHAEDO*

In the *Phaedo* Socrates is concerned to tell us not only what kind of soul we have, but also its value and what the implications of his view are for the way that we ought to live our lives. This is to say that there is a moral point underlying Socrates' arguments. If we miss this point we miss a great deal about what the arguments themselves are aiming at. Plato's *Phaedo* is a dialogue narrating the last hours and final discussion of Socrates' life. Socrates has no need to worry about assemblies and the swaying opinions of large gatherings of Athenian men. He is alone with all but a few of his intimate friends. The central event of the dialogue is not the death of Socrates, but the struggle to overcome the *fear* of death. And right up until the end of his life the character Socrates attempts to lure his friends with the fragrance of philosophy. In the *Apology* Socrates introduced the theme of philosophy as "care of the soul"; in the *Phaedo* this theme finds its consummation (cf. 107Cff).

But why is it important to prove the soul is immortal? Do we have any clue as to what value Socrates assigns to his arguments or, we might say, what *motivated* him to want to prove to his friends that the soul is immortal? In the dramatic context of the *Phaedo* the arguments for immortality come about as a result of Socrates accepting the challenge to stand on 'trial' for a second time. This time he stands on trial not before the Athenians but before his friends with the task of explaining his claims about philosophy. He has to defend his position that a philosopher will calmly meet his death since philosophy itself is a preparation for death. In other words, Socrates has to explain the premise underlying his argument that a philosopher will be the one to have good cheer (θαρρεῖν) and be hopeful towards (εὔελπις εἶναι) death, while all the while refusing suicide and death unless it be forced upon him (63E-64A).

Surely, Socrates has to defend his belief in the immortal soul if he is going to uphold his conception of philosophy as *the practice of death*. He says that belief in the immortal soul and its future happiness is a risk or a hazard, but that it is a noble risk (καλὸς γὰρ ὁ κίνδυνος) and one worthwhile taking. At the very end of his pictorial representation of the afterlife to Simmias and Cebes, he admits that he cannot prove what he has just represented to them, but nevertheless that the image has merit:

> No sensible man would insist that these things are as I have described them, but I think it is fitting for a man to risk the belief—for the risk is a noble one (καλὸς γὰρ ὁ κίνδυνος)—that this, or something like this, is true about our souls and their dwelling places, since the soul is evidently immortal, and a man should repeat this to himself as if it were an incantation, which is why I have been prolonging my tale. 114DE

Belief in the immortality of the soul is so important that one should repeat this teaching as though it were a spell to be chanted continuously. Again, why is this belief important? And are there any other reasons that we have not explicitly referred to that Socrates might have for wanting his friends to be convinced by these arguments? I think that there are three other motives or ends that Socrates thinks he achieves by his arguments; three reasons why the arguments for immortality are important arguments to make.

First of all, Socrates presents himself as though he wants to convince his friends of the argument for personal immortality because he thinks it is true. We cannot brush aside this fact. He says as much during the interlude wherein he warns them against misology or becoming sceptical of the value of rational argumentation (89D-91D). Socrates is forthright about the fact that he thinks the truth is more valuable than deliberately believing in a deception about the soul's immortality, however noble such a deception may turn out to be. "For I am thinking," Socrates mused, "that if what I say is true, it is a fine thing to be convinced; if, on the other hand, nothing exists after death . . . my folly will not continue to exist along with me—that would be a bad thing—but will come to an end in a short time" (91AB).

Secondly, belief in the immortal soul can have positive moral effects on its adherents. Believing that the soul is immortal can motivate one to practice moral virtue. Socrates pointed out to Simmias and Cebes that if death were really the end then there would be a remarkable equality between the good and the bad. Neither would the good be rewarded, nor would the wicked be punished for their deeds if death were the end of human consciousness. This sort of equality between the good and the bad might potentially lead to harmful moral consequences, and the neglect of one's own education. For if death were actually an escape from one's own deeds, then death would hold out for the wicked an easy opportunity to escape the consequences that justice seems to require. The wicked could go free without punishment, without repentance. On the other hand, Socrates seems keenly aware of how belief in the immortal soul can strengthen one's motive for becoming wise and virtuous: "But now that the soul appears to be immortal, there is no escape from evil or salvation for it except by becoming as good and as wise as possible" (107CD).

The second reason leads to the third. Belief in the soul's immortality is valuable because it can help a person attain happiness in this life and the next. Throughout the dialogue Socrates constantly refers to the philosopher's ability to have good cheer (θαρρεῖν) in the face of death. Certainly after death the philosopher gains great happiness in the company of gods and the Forms, but even in this life the philosopher lives better than those who act as though only material causes exist (98DE, 118A). In saying this I am not suggesting that the philosopher practices virtue because of the outcome of a calculated cost-benefit analysis of the results of virtue. Socrates repeatedly rejects such a notion in the most stringent terms (69Aff). No, virtue has its own intrinsic rewards even if its benefits happen to extend into the next life as well. Thus in life, at the moment of departure, and after death Socrates holds out philosophy as the doorway to happiness.

I think that all of Socrates' comments on the soul in the *Phaedo* are to be understood with a view to each of the above considerations. Socrates wants to convince his friends of the truth of the conclusion of his argument; he thinks belief in the immortal soul helps to provide a rationale for practicing *katharsis* and the pursuit of virtue; and this cultivation of virtue in its turn results in noble action at death and happiness in the bodiless state that follows death. Socrates, no doubt, wants to convince his friends of the doctrine of the immortal soul because he thinks it true.

We have come to the end of our study. By separating out two conceptions of the soul in the *Phaedo* we have gained a better understanding of Socrates' argumentation about the soul as well as the total view of the soul itself as presented in this and other dialogues. The history of the philosophical and theological traditions that developed over the subsequent centuries found in

Plato's thoughts a wellspring of ideas. Plato's teaching served to give life to the emerging doctrines of the soul that, formed under the influence of both Hebrew and Classical Greek thought, were brought together in the teachings of the Christian Church. And in relation to that history, this was but a prelude.

NOTES

1. Also, in the *Phaedo* Socrates sometimes speaks as though the human is a composite being comprised of a body and a soul (79B, 94B); at other times he appears to speak as though body and soul are both subordinate to the ruling of a third super-ego that even governs the activities of the soul (66BC, 67E, 88B). Robinson comments on the way that Socrates sometimes does and sometimes does not speak as though the soul were the locus of the self. On 66B and 67E he writes: "Once more the soul and its possessor seem to be distinguished, as also apparently at 64E8-65A2. How seriously this is to be taken is hard to say. If it is taken at its face value, the true self will be some sort of super-Ego beyond soul and body, and this will stand in direct conflict with the view of the self as the soul. Be this as it may, what is quite certain is that Socrates wants to flout the greater part of tradition by maintaining that the self or person is definitely *not* the body." *TMR*, 32.

2. This conclusion is similar to that reached by Martha Beck in her study of the arguments of the *Phaedo* where she sets out to argue the following: "The thesis to be defended here is that Socrates' positions in these three arguments [in the *Phaedo*] become progressively more complex, more comprehensive and more systematic. When the arguments are read in the order presented, each discussion of the immortality of the soul leads to unresolved problems which, in turn, are addressed immediately and directly in the next discussion." *ibid.*, 2.

3. As mentioned, for instance, in David Ross' work, *ibid.*, 1–10.

Bibliography

Beck, Martha C. *Plato's Self-Corrective Development of the Concepts of Soul, Forms and Immortality in Three Arguments of the* Phaedo. Lewiston, New York: The Edwin Mellen Press, Ltd., 1999.
Bostock, David. *Plato's* Phaedo. Oxford: Clarendon Press, 1986.
Brandwood, Leonard. *A Word Index to Plato*. Leeds: W.S. Maney & Sons Ltd., 1976.
——. "Stylometry and Chronology" pp. 90–120 in *The Cambridge Companion to Plato*. Ed. Richard Kraut. Cambridge: CUP, 1992.
Bremmer, Jan, N. *The Rise and Fall of the Afterlife*. London: Routledge, 2002.
Brickhouse, Thomas C. and Nicholas D. Smith. *Plato's Socrates*. Oxford: OUP, 1994.
——. *The Philosophy of Socrates*. Boulder, Colorado: Westview Press, 2000.
——. *The Trial and Executions of Socrates: Sources and Controversies*. Oxford: OUP, 2002.
Burnet, John. Edited with Notes. *Plato's* Euthyphro, Apology *of Socrates and* Crito. Oxford: Clarendon Press, 1977.
——. Edited with Notes. *Plato's* Phaedo, Oxford: Clarendon Press, 1911.
——. The Socratic Doctrine of the Soul, Second Annual Philosophical Lecture: Henriette Hertz Trust. Proceedings of the British Academy 7 (1916): 235–259.
Carey, Christopher. *Trials From Classical Athens*. London: Routledge, 1997.
Chadwick, H. *Early Christian Thought and the Classical Tradition: Studies in Justin, Clement, and Origen*. Oxford: OUP, 1966.
Chantriane, Pierre. *Dictionnaire Etymologique de la Langue Grecque: histoire des mots*, Volume 1. Paris: Editions Klincksieck, 1983.
Claus, David B. *Toward the Soul: An Inquiry into the Meaning of psyche before Plato*. London: Yale University Press, 1981.
Copi, Irvin M. and Carl Cohen. *Introduction to Logic*, 10th edition. Upper Saddle River, NJ: Prentice Hall, 1988.
Craig, Leon Harold. *The War Lover: A Study in Plato's* Republic. Toronto: University of Toronto Press, 1996.

Bibliography

Cullmann, Oscar. *Immortality of the Soul or Resurrection of the Dead? The Witness of the New Testament*. London: The Epworth Press, 1958.

Dempsey, T. *The Delphic Oracle: Its Early History, Influence and Fall*. New York: Benjamin Blom, Inc., 1972.

Dover, Kenneth. *Symposuim*. Edited with notes. Cambridge: CUP, 2002.

Duke, E.A. et. al. eds. *Platonis Opera: Tomus I*. Oxonii: E Typographeo Clarendoniano, 1995.

Gallop, David. *Phaedo*. Translation with notes. Oxford: Clarendon Press, 1975.

Grube, G.M.A. *Phaedo*. Tranlsator. Notes and edited by John Cooper in *The Complete Works of Plato*. Indianapolis: Hackett, 1997.

Guthrie, W.K.C. *A History of Greek Philosophy*, Volume 4. New York: Cambridge University Press, 1975.

———. *The Greek Philosophers: From Thales to Aristotle*. New York: Harper & Row Publishers, 1960

Homer. *Iliad*. Trans. Richard Lattimore. Chicago: University of Chicago Press, 1961.

Klein, Jacob. *A commentary on Plato's* Meno. Chapel Hill, NC: The University of North Carolina Press, 1965.

Liddell, H.G., R. Scott and H. S. Jones, *A Revised Greek-English Lexicon*. Oxford: Clarendon Press, 1968.

Robinson, T.M. *Plato's Psychology*, second edition. Toronto: University of Toronto Press, 1995.

Ross, David. *Plato's Theory of Ideas*. Oxford: Clarendon Press, 1961.

Rowe, C.J. *Phaedrus*. Translation and Commentary. Warminister, Wiltshire, UK: Aris and Phillips, Ltd., 1986.

Sharples, R.W. *Meno*. Translation with Introduction and Commentary.Warminister, Wiltshire, UK: Aris and Phillips, Ltd., 1985.

Shorey, Paul. *Republic*. Translation with Introduction and Notes. Cambridge, Massachusetts: Harvard University Press, 1937.

Strauss, Leo. *The City and Man*. Chicago: University of Chicago Press, 1978.

Vlastos, Gregory. *Socrates: Ironist and Moral Philosopher*. New York: Cornell University Press, 1991.

West, Thomas G, and Grace Starry West. *Four Texts on Socrates: Plato's* Euthyphro, Apology, *and* Crito *and Aristophanes'* Clouds. Ithaca: Cornell University Press, 1984.

Westerink, L.G. *The Greek Commentaries on Plato's* Phaedo: *Volume 1: Olympiodorus*. New York: North-Holland Publishing Co., 1976.

Index

Achilles, 42
Albinus, 5
Alcestis, 42
Anaxagoras, 27
Aristotle, 22

Beck, Martha, 57n2
Bostock, David, 37n15
Burnet, John, 6, 18, 35n2, 36n8, 38n20,

care of the soul, 14–15, 34, 54
Cebes, 1, 15, 19–20, 22-23, 25–29, 36n7, 47, 55–56
creation *ex nihilo*, 22

Diotima, 41

Echecrates, 15, 28
Eryximachus, 40

forms, 23–32, 34-35, 36n10, 37n14, 41–42, 47, 52, 54

Gallop, David, 37n12, 38n20
Glaucon, 48

Iamblichus, 7

Klein, Jacob, 35n3, 38n20

Lysias, 45

materialism, 15
Meno, 39–40
mind, 36n8, 37n12, 49
misology, 16, 55

Olympiodorus, 7

perplexity, 40
Phaedo, 15, 28
Phaedrus, 45
purification (*katharsis*), 1, 15, 18, 31–32, 38n20–21, 56

recollection, doctrine of, 40, 50, 54
Robinson, T. M., 18, 18n5, 38n21, 57n1
Ross, David, 50n1

St. Augustine, 36n5, 38n22
Simmias, 1, 12, 15, 17, 19, 23, 25, 36n7, 55–56

teleology, 27

virtue, 3, 17, 31, 34–35, 39–40, 49, 53, 56
Vlastos, Gregory, 6

www.ingramcontent.com/pod-product-compliance
Lightning Source LLC
Chambersburg PA
CBHW052051300426
44117CB00012B/2084